LEGENDS OF WARFARE
AVIATION

Legacy Hornets

Boeing's F/A-18 A-D Hornets of the USN and USMC

BRAD ELWARD

Schiffer Publishing Ltd
4880 Lower Valley Road • Atglen, PA 19310

Designed by Justin Watkinson
Type set in Impact/Minion Pro/Univers LT Std

ISBN: 978-0-7643-5434-2
Printed in China

Published by Schiffer Publishing, Ltd.
4880 Lower Valley Road
Atglen, PA 19310
Phone: (610) 593-1777; Fax: (610) 593-2002
E-mail: Info@schifferbooks.com
www.schifferbooks.com

For our complete selection of fine books on this and related subjects, please visit our website at www.schifferbooks.com. You may also write for a free catalog.

Schiffer Publishing's titles are available at special discounts for bulk purchases for sales promotions or premiums. Special editions, including personalized covers, corporate imprints, and excerpts, can be created in large quantities for special needs. For more information, contact the publisher.

We are always looking for people to write books on new and related subjects. If you have an idea for a book, please contact us at proposals@schifferbooks.com.

Contents

Introduction

The Boeing F/A-18 Hornet represents the blending of two missions–fighter and attack–into what is now commonly known as the strike fighter. A multi-mission platform, the F/A-18 can perform virtually all missions, ranging from purely fighter to attack to maritime strike, and can deliver the majority of today's air-to-air and air-to-ground weaponry. The aircraft emerged from Northrop's YF-17 Cobra design submitted for the United States Air Force's Lightweight Fighter Competition in the early 1970s. The competition sought a complimentary platform to serve side-by-side with the McDonnell Douglas F-15 Eagle, the latest in air superiority fighters. Although losing the Air Force competition, the YF-17 provided the foundation for the aircraft the Navy would develop into the F/A-18 Hornet.

The F/A-18A entered US Navy and Marine Corps service in 1983, and quickly provided its worth as a capable, reliable multi-mission aircraft replacing the McDonnell Douglas F-4 Phantom II fighter-bomber, LTV A-7 Corsair II light attack aircraft, and the aging McDonnell Douglas A-4 Skyhawk light attack aircraft. Early model Hornets were extremely effective dogfighters and even using optical bombing methods were outperforming their A-7 predecessors. Hornets also gave fleet commanders much-needed mission flexibility within the air wing, while proving easy for new pilots to learn and routinely scoring high marks in recovering aboard the carrier. Early Hornets also marked their presence on the international scene, with sales to Canada, Australia, and Spain.

Although just entering fleet service, work had already begun on upgrades to the Hornet that would culminate with the F/A-18C/D and later the F/A-18C/D Night Attack variants. These versions of the Hornet offered a significant increase in capabilities and are often considered the aircraft the Hornet was supposed to be from the outset. These variants incorporated the new APG-73 radar, a new electronic countermeasures system, improved computers, unrated engines, and the ability to conduct strike operations day or night. They also introduced the ability to carry the new AIM-120 AMRAAM radar-guided medium-range missile, the AGM-84 Harpoon, and, in conjunction with the new AAS-38A/B laser designator, a variety of laser guided munitions. The two-seat Hornet, dubbed the F/A-18D, assumed a new tactical role and replaced the Marine Corps Grumman A-6 Intruders in the all-weather strike role, and became quite effective in the Forward Air Control-Airborne (FAC-A) mission targeting for other aircraft. F/A-18D crews later acquired an effective reconnaissance capability through the Advanced Targeting and Reconnaissance System (ATARS). International sales of the F/A-18C/D followed, with Switzerland, Kuwait, Finland, and Malaysia purchasing aircraft.

Hornets were heavily involved in Operation Desert Storm, and even scored two air-to-air kills against Iraqi MiGs, but their true value—in flexibility and reliability—came during the air operations against Bosnia and Kosovo during the mid-1990s and the large overseas contingency operations of the early and mid-2000s, namely Operation Enduring Freedom (OEF) in Afghanistan, and Operation Iraqi Freedom (OIF) in Iraq. In these wars, Hornets, now capable of carrying both laser-guided and GPS-guided munitions, became the platform of choice. Indeed, OIF has been termed "The Hornet War," in reference to the large number of F/A-18s (US Navy, US Marine Corps, Canadian, and Australian) involved.

Today, the Hornet, now referred to as the Legacy Hornet due to the emergence of its big brother, the F/A-18E/F Super Hornet, is in full sustainment mode, as both the Navy and Marine Corps, as well as its international operators, work to keep them flying until the next generation of strike fighters arrive. As of early 2017, the Navy operates only a handful of Legacy Hornets—all from its East Coast base at NAS Oceana, Virginia. The remaining Legacy Hornets are flown by the Marine Corps and are being worked hard. Older F/A-18A Legacy Hornets have either been retired or significantly upgraded to F/A-18A+ and A++ standards (comparable with the F/A-18C), and feature the latest technologies such as the Joint Helmet Mounted Cueing System (JHMCS) and the high off-bore site (HOBS) AIM-9X Sidewinder missile.

The Legacy Hornets in American service are scheduled to be retired towards the end of the 2020s or early 2030s, with the Marine Corps' F/A-18D squadrons being the last to operate this great aircraft. With a career likely to ultimately span more than forty-five years, the Legacy Hornet has proven itself time and time again as an effective strike fighter able to perform the entire spectrum of missions, many within the same flight. This flexibility has become a hallmark trait of the Legacy Hornet, and its Super Hornet successor, and has made it incredibly valuable to air wing commanders, allowing them to surge to meet the operation needs at hand. During the 1960s and 1970s, wing commanders were constrained by smaller numbers of highly specialized aircraft that were not always available for use when their specialties were not in play. With the Hornet, the entire tactical air wing was available for all missions. This meant that air wings, whether Navy carrier-based or Marine Corps land-based, could become smaller, while at the same time becoming more lethal.

The F/A-18 Hornet is the first aircraft specifically designed as a strike fighter to perform both fighter and light attack missions. Designed in the mid-1970s, the Hornet is still serving in the US Navy and Marine Corps as well as the air forces of seven foreign nations. *US Navy*

CHAPTER 1

Origins of the Hornet

The Boeing F/A-18 Hornet arose from a United States Air Force (USAF) effort to develop a low-cost fighter as a complement to the complex and expensive McDonnell Douglas F-15 Eagle air superiority fighter. As the F-15 program's costs rose and concern was expressed that the Soviet Union was numerically eliminating the US technical advantage, the Air Force revisited the Light Weight Fighter (LWF) concept of the 1950s as a complement, rather than as an alternative, to the F-15. On August 24, 1971, the Air Force announced a fly-off to evaluate two yet-to-be submitted LWF prototypes. The Navy was told to monitor the LWF program and consider whether either competitor could be made suitable for carrier operations.

On December 31, the Request for Proposal (RFP) was released followed by the model contract on January 6, 1972, marking the start of the LWF program. Five companies submitted proposals and in mid-March the results were announced with Boeing, General Dynamics, and Northrop's offerings all making the final cut. After further requirements analysis, the General Dynamics model was selected as the most desirable, followed by the Northrop design. On April 13, 1972, the General Dynamics and the Northrop submissions were selected for the fly-off and each company was given funds for two prototypes.

The Need Emerges in the Navy

The Navy had pursued its own air superiority fighter, the Grumman F-14 Tomcat. The Tomcat, like the F-15, represented the "high-end" of the fighter spectrum, both in cost and performance. The Tomcat was based around the powerful AWG-9 radar and the long-range AIM-54 Phoenix air-to-air missile, which was designed to counter long-range Soviet bombers and their long-range missiles.

The Navy soon realized that it too needed a low-cost companion for the sophisticated Tomcat, but one that would also replace the aging McDonnell Douglas A-4 Skyhawk, Vought A-7 Corsair II, and the F-4 Phantom II in the light attack role.

In September 1973, the Navy issued a formal RFP seeking combined air-to-air and air-to-ground platform, termed VFA-X for Naval Fighter-Attack, Experimental. In mid-1974, however, Congress abruptly cancelled the VFA-X program and directed that "the development of this aircraft make maximum use of the Air Force lightweight fighter and Air Combat Fighter technology and hardware" in a new program titled "Navy Air Combat Fighter." Unlike its Air Force counterpart, however, the NACF would be capable of air-to-air and air-to-ground missions. In accordance with the Congressional directive, naval aviators evaluated both competitors for possible carrier usage. By late September 1974, Northrop joined forces with McDonnell Douglas and General Dynamics sought affiliation with Ling-Temco-Vought (LTV), both notable aerospace companies who had already produced successful Navy jets.

The YF-16

The YF-16 (Model 401) was a leap in technology by way of its analog fly-by-wire (FBW) flight control system. Small and maneuverable, it featured a single Pratt & Whitney F100-PE-100 23,500-lb. thrust (104.78 kN) engine, a derivative of that used by the F-15, and could carry a 13,200-lb. (6,000 kg) external load. With afterburner, the YF-16 was projected to have a 1.28:1 combat thrust-to-weight ratio. In addition to its revolutionary flight control system, it featured a unique reclined pilot seat and a side-column controller, rather than the conventional center stick between the legs.

The YF-17

Northrop's YF-17 submission drew on the company's already successful F-5/T-38 family designs from the 1950s and early 1960s. In 1965, Northrop began the N-300 program; essentially an F-5 with a stretched fuselage, two engines, and the addition of small leading-edge extensions, called LEXs, which created a vortex over the upper wing surfaces that separated the boundary layer air and greatly improved maneuverability at high angles of attack. Long, oval shaped inlet ducts positioned far forward on the fuselage fed air into the engines.

As the N-300 evolved, the LEX was enlarged and the engine inlets were moved even further back under the LEX, although still not as far as they are on the Hornet. The design retained the single vertical stabilizer of the F-5, but featured all-moving stabilators mounted below midline. In 1968, however, the single vertical stabilizer was split into twin vertical stabilizers, each about one-half the size of the original stabilizer, which canted outward at an almost forty-five degree angle so that they would remain in the free-stream air flow.

What resulted from these efforts was a near-Mach 2 Model P-530 aircraft with both an air-to-air and air-to-ground capability and weighing approximately 40,000 lbs. Although it gained little interest, the LWF competition breathed new life into the program, as Northrop stripped the P-530 of its air-to-ground capability and re-designated it as the P-600 for the competition. Reflecting the emphasis on air combat, the gun was moved from underneath the fuselage, where it was better suited to strafing, and placed in the nose where it would function better in aerial combat. The YF-17 also received the new GE 14,400-lb. thrust (64.21 kN) YJ101-GE-100 turbofan engines but mounted close together to minimize possible asymmetrical forces in the event of engine failure by one of the turbojets. The YF-17's first flight occurred at Edwards AFB on June 9, 1974.

LWF Becomes the Air Combat Fighter (ACF)

In April 1974, the USAF announced it was now considering full-scale development and eventual production "of an ACF-type aircraft," a move that significantly raised the stakes of the competition, now termed the Air Combat Fighter (ACF). In September, the Air Force announced that it would produce a minimum of 650 ACF, which meant the winner would receive a full production contract and potentially huge foreign sales. Although initially scheduled to last more than a year, the time table for the ACF competition was drastically shortened and both contractors were instructed to complete their testing by mid-December 1974. The reason for this urgency was simple–several European countries were also interested in finding a new fighter to replace their aging fleets. These countries formed a consortium and were considering the two American ACF prototypes, as well as several European models, and would make a decision in January 1975.

On January 13, 1975, the USAF announced the YF-16 as winner of the ACF program fly-off, citing the YF-16's slightly better performance (maneuverability, roll-rate, and range), its projected lower cost versus the YF-17, and its commonality with the F-15's engine.

The Navy Is Left with Little Choice

Although disappointed, the Navy continued to evaluate both aircraft to determine which aircraft better suited its operational needs. Although General Dynamics had teamed up with veteran Navy designer LTV, the revised YF-16 proposal was proving a difficult sell. The Navy had significant concerns about the ability to convert the aircraft for carrier operations without substantially diminishing its capabilities as a lightweight fighter and also liked the YF-17's two-engine design, its multi-mission adaptability, and inherent room for growth.

On May 2, 1975, the Navy announced it would develop a derivative of the YF-17 to be known as the F-18 Naval Air Combat Fighter (NACF). McDonnell Douglas, now designated the primary manufacturer for the aircraft because of its vast experience with carrier aircraft, was awarded a $4.4 million contract to continue work until a formal agreement could be reached.

The McDonnell Douglas F-4 Phantom II was designed in the late 1950s to serve as the frontline fighter/interceptor for the United States Air Force, Navy, and Marine Corps. During the Vietnam War, the Phantom II was more often employed as a fighter-bomber and was many times called upon to dogfight against North Vietnamese MiGs. The aircraft proved difficult to fight against the more maneuverable Soviet and Chinese-built MiGs. *Naval Aviation Museum*

The Grumman F-14 Tomcat was the Navy's answer to the fighter deficiencies of the Vietnam War. The F/A-18 was intended to compliment the Tomcat, as well as other light attack aircraft. Here an F-14D Tomcat assigned to VF-213 *Black Lions* flies in a loose formation with an F/A-18A+ Hornet assigned to VFA-204 *River Rattlers* during a training mission over New Orleans. *US Navy*

The McDonnell Douglas F-15 Eagle gave the United States Air Force a dedicated fighter second to none until the introduction of the Lockheed Martin F-22 Raptor. Despite the Eagle's tremendous capabilities, its costs led the Air Force to begin considering a lower-cost stablemate, which led to the Lightweight Fighter (LWF) Competition between the General Dynamics YF-16 Falcon and Northrop YF-17 Cobra. *Ted Carlson*

The YF-16's cockpit had excellent visibility for the pilot, the aircraft was extremely maneuverable, and it shared a common engine with the F-15A Eagle. *Northrop*

Northrop's YF-17 offering represented the maturation of a long line of designs dating back to the 1950s. The YF-17 was highly maneuverable and capable of operating at high angles of attack. *Northrop*

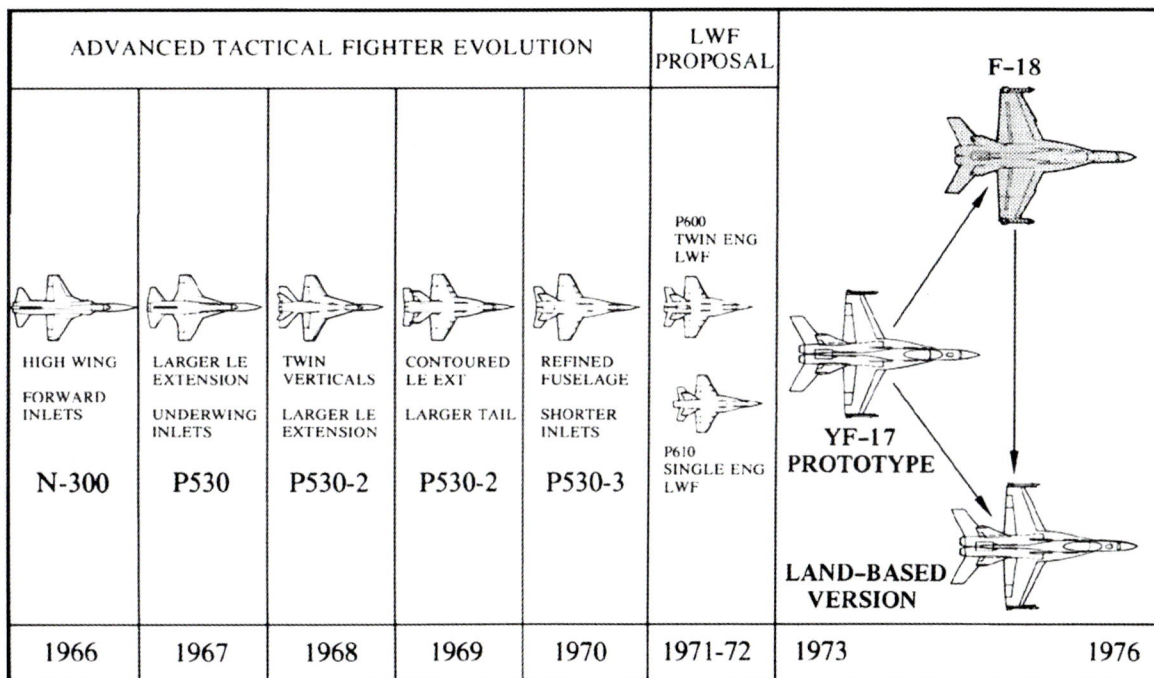

This chart shows the progression and evolution of the N-300 to the YF-17. *Northrop Grumman*

ADVANCED TACTICAL FIGHTER EVOLUTION					LWF PROPOSAL		
							F-18
					P600 TWIN ENG LWF		
HIGH WING FORWARD INLETS	LARGER LE EXTENSION UNDERWING INLETS	TWIN VERTICALS LARGER LE EXTENSION	CONTOURED LE EXT LARGER TAIL	REFINED FUSELAGE SHORTER INLETS			
					P610 SINGLE ENG LWF	**YF-17 PROTOTYPE**	
N-300	P530	P530-2	P530-2	P530-3			**LAND-BASED VERSION**
1966	1967	1968	1969	1970	1971-72	1973	1976

The F/A-18 shares many attributes with the YF-17, including the canted tailfins, leading edge extensions (LEX), and "D"-shaped engine inlets. *Northrop*

The Navy sought to complement the F-14 fighter and to replace several light attack platforms, including the Vought A-7 Corsair II, shown here, the F-4 Phantom II, and the McDonnell Douglas A-4 Skyhawk. The A-7 served well in Vietnam and earned a reputation of flying long distances and delivering large payloads. *Naval Aviation Museum*

The two LWF competitors, General Dynamics and Northrop, each teamed with well-respected manufacturers of successful naval aircraft. Northrop teamed with McDonnell Douglas and General Dynamics teamed with LVT. The YF-16 is shown here with the Vought/LTV A-7 Corsair II, and F-8 Crusader. *LVT via the Naval Aviation Museum*

One of the two YF-17 prototypes (72-1570) is shown here at NAS Lemoore with "A-18 Prototype" markings shortly after the LWF Competition. *Northrop via Don Logan*

Northrop developed a wooden mock-up of the YF-17 in 1972, and later modified it as a two-seat platform. Note the AIM-7 Sparrow missiles on the wingtip rails. *Don Logan*

A predecessor of the P-600, which became the YF-17, the P530 cockpit featured old-style dials and gauges but still offered modern technology, including a Heads-Up Display (HUD) and Radar Warning Receiver (RWR). *Don Logan*

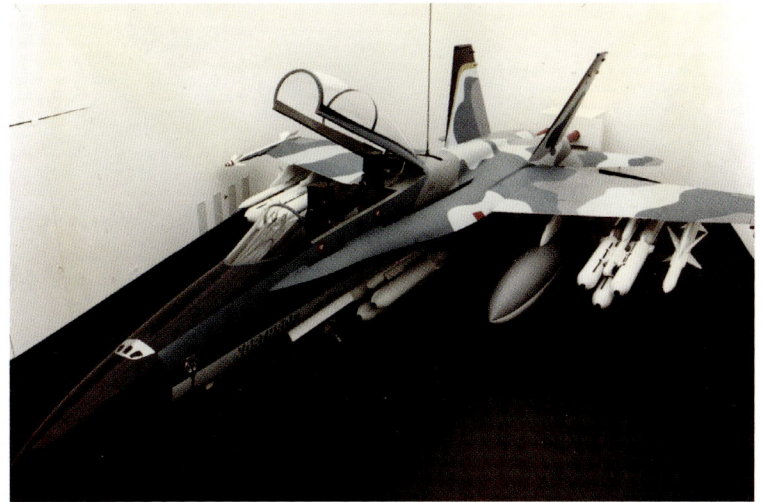

Once the YF-17 became the carrier-based F-18/A-18, McDonnell Douglas took over the role of primary contractor, while Northrop manufactured the aft fuselage section. *Northrop via Naval Aviation Museum*

Northrop marketed a land-based version of the Hornet called the F-18L. *Northrop Grumman*

CHAPTER 2

Design, Test, and Evaluation

An artist rendition shows the F-18 fighter and A-18 attack variants originally proposed for the program. The aircraft was to be reconfigurable by exchanging a few internal system boxes. The advent of the Hughes APG-65 radar, which permitted both air-to-air and air-to-ground coverage, meant that all missions could now be performed by a single aircraft and led to the F/A-18 designation. *Boeing*

On January 22, 1976, a $1.43 billion seven-year Full-Scale Development (FSD) contract was signed calling for eleven Research & Development aircraft and specifying the first flight before July 1978. Three versions of the Hornet were planned—the F-18 fighter for the Navy and Marine Corps; the A-18 attack variant for the Navy; and the TF-18, a dual-seat trainer for Navy and Marine Corps training. The TF-18 would also retain a basic armament capability.

McDonnell Douglas and Northrop built the F-18 using a 60/40 split; McDonnell Douglas manufactured the wings, stabilators, and forward fuselage area, while Northrop produced the center and aft fuselage sections, and the vertical stabilizers. The rear fuselage assemblies were shipped to St. Louis where they were mated with the wings and forward fuselage, and final test flights were conducted.

On March 1, 1977, the F-18 was named "Hornet," highlighting the aircraft's ability to "strike rapidly and produce a sharp sting." The initial contract called for 780 F-18s and A-18s. The first F-18 (160775) was rolled out at McDonnell Douglas' St. Louis facility on September 13, 1978, and made its maiden flight on November 18. Piloted by McDonnell Douglas Chief Test Pilot John E. "Jack" Krings, the fifty minute flight from St. Louis to Springfield, Illinois, and back, reached a top speed of 300 knots and an altitude of 24,000 feet.

The F-18 began flight tests at the Naval Air Test Center (NATC) Patuxent River in January 1979, which lasted through October 1982. Most flight testing was conducted at Patuxent River under a system known as the Principal Site Concept, which incorporated substantial input from the Navy and allowed McDonnell Douglas more time to incorporate modifications and fix deficiencies. It also kept all the Hornets together at one test location, reducing logistics problems. All eleven FSD aircraft were assigned to the flight test program, with each aircraft assuming the specific program duties.

Test Flights Unveil Issues

Many expected the flight test phase to proceed without a hitch given the extensive testing done on the YF-17. Yet as with many aircraft programs the F-18 had glitches to be resolved. In fact, some issues were of such degree that the wing and the tail section had to be partially redesigned. Virtually all of these "deficiencies" were resolved during the flight test program and modifications were incorporated into the production aircraft.

One of the most significant deficiencies concerned the Hornet's roll-rate, which worsened at low altitude and higher speeds, especially near the speed of sound. The cause was confirmed as the outer wings being flexed in high load situations and the Sidewinders, when attached on their wingtip stations, imparting too much roll dampening. Solutions included strengthening the wing spar and eliminating the dogtooth on the leading-edge wing flap, allowing the latter to extend the full distance of the leading edge flap. The ailerons were extended out to the wingtip to provide more deflection and the leading-edge flaps were split so they could operate independently. Composite skins were thickened, thereby improving wing rigidity and reducing outer wing panel twist.

The Sidewinder launch rails were moved forward by five inches and angled to an even sharper nose-down incidence. These modifications brought the roll rate up to an acceptable 220 degrees per second rate, still short of the initial 280 degrees per second rate established by the Navy. FSD F-8 received the first complete wing modifications and all Hornets manufactured after No.17 were built with the redesigned wings. Aircraft Nos.15 and 16 were completed with new wings out of production sequence, and aircraft Nos.10–14 were retrofitted with new wings.

Related to the roll rate problem, the acceleration time from Mach 0.8 through Mach 1.6 was even less than the 120 seconds of the F-4, an aircraft the F/A-18 was to replace. Flight control changes reduced acceleration times to less than 120 seconds, although not as low as the required eighty seconds.

Flight tests also revealed the A-18 suffered a 10–12 percent deficiency in range payload when flying in attack profiles. Navy requirements called for a range of 444 nm (820.8 km) when configured as a fighter and 635 nm (1,174.8 km) when configured as an attack aircraft. Initial flight tests, however, placed these figures at 400 and 580 nm (740.3 and 1,073.4 km) respectively. The F-18 in the fighter escort role still had a greater range than the F-4 Phantom II it replaced and was judged superior to that aircraft.

In mid-1982, the Pentagon cleared the Hornet for full-scale production as a fighter. However, due to range limitations, VX-5's Operational Evaluation (OpEval) report recommended against the F/A-18 as a replacement for the A-7 in the attack role, citing range and endurance deficiencies. Realistically, since the attack and fighter variants had merged into one platform due to radar advancements, the decision really involved how many planes would be produced. It also meant an end to the quest for a strike fighter, as the Hornet would be relegated to primarily fighter missions and the Navy would have been left searching for yet another aircraft.

Some Navy officials responded sharply to the VX-5 OpEval report, noting that the flight tests were based on faulty flight profiles. Capt. J.W. Partington, Commanding Officer of VFA-125, later commented, "We must stop utilizing the fuel flow gauge of the A-7E as a measure of the Hornet's fuel specifics. If we tie an F/A-18 to the wing of an A-7 on its standard mission profile, the Corsair will win every fuel gauge comparison, although not by the large margin commonly assumed. If, however, one reverses the roles by tying the A-7 to the wing of the Hornet on its optimum mission profile, the competition will cease at the take-off end of the runway as the F/A-18 becomes a dot in the Corsair's windscreen." These comments were backed up by numbers accumulated by VFA-125 as it worked with the Hornet.

In a 1982 *Aviation Week & Space Technology* article, the author referenced a November 13, letter sent by Cdr. Jerry D. Palmer, Commander of VFA-125, to VADM Robert F. Schoultz, Deputy Chief of Naval Operations (Air Warfare), which compared a 600 nm (1,111.2 km) strike by self-escorted F/A-18s with a force of A-7Es escorted by F-14s and found that the F/A-18 strike group required less tanking. The F/A-18 group required 50,000 lbs. (22,679.6 kg) of fuel while the A-7/F-14 group required 52,000 lbs. (23,586.8 kg) of fuel. The article also noted that during a deployment to Yuma in early 1982, F/A-18s were able to maneuver for a simulated rear aspect gun or AIM-9 shot on an F-14 in twenty of thirty-four engagements, while the F-14 was never able to obtain a simulated firing solution on an F/A-18.

To put the range issue to rest once and for all, SECNAV John Lehman ordered the Navy to make a test flight. Although not a clear vindication of the Hornet's range because of the need to return to base prematurely, the post flight analysis of the onboard data provided meaningful results that identified why the Hornet had deviated from its expected fuel use plan and supported the aircraft's range capabilities. The flight was repeated the following day by one of VX-5's junior officers: "The fuel numbers again were matching the predicted fuel flow and fuel state throughout the profile including after the simulated combat turns." When the Pentagon hearing finally came in early 1983, Lehman gave his blessings and asked that the Hornet be placed into full production. The Hornet was approved for use in the attack role on March 17, 1983.

Other mechanical causes for the range deficiency were also discovered during testing. For example, the leading-edge flaps were found to extend down a few degrees too far and the boundary layer air discharge slots (referred to as LEX slots) increased drag. The flaps were adjusted and the LEX slots partially filled, leaving only a small slot aft of the cockpit to funnel fuselage bleed air away from the intakes. Approximately eighty percent of the length of the slots was filled beginning with the eighth FSD F-18A. Unfortunately, the turbulent air caused by the elimination of these slots contributed largely to the fatigue problems experienced later with the Hornet's vertical stabilizers, which led to cracks at the attachment points and temporarily grounded the Hornet fleet. Fatigue issues were remedied by adding four-inch metal cleats at several of the attachment locations in late 1984, and by adding a small fence at the top of each LEX near the leading edge beginning in May 1988, to broaden the vortices which had caused the fatigue. The LEX fences even improved controllability at high angles of attack.

F/A-18 No.3 (160777) completed seventy land catapult launches and 120 arrested landings at Patuxent River, before departing for USS *America* (CV-66) for initial sea trials from October 30, through November 3. The Hornet made thirty-two launches and traps, seventeen touch-and-go landings, and logged approximately fourteen hours of flight time. The Hornet had posted approach speeds of approximately 140 knots (161.3 mph) although requirements called for a 115- to 125-knot (132.5 to 144 mph) approach speed with no wind over deck (WOD). The solution was found by configuring the leading-edge flaps to thirty degrees and the trailing-edge flaps to forty-five degrees of extension during landing, and coupled with software modifications, reduced the approach speed to 134 knots where it remains today.

This right side and undercarriage view provide an exceptional opportunity to see the F/A-18's contour lines. The aircraft has a strong resemblance to the YF-17, but shares no common dimensions with that aircraft. Notice this image was taken prior to the addition of the fence plate on the Leading Edge Extension (LEX) in 1988. *Boeing*

A1-F18AC-NFM-000

TANK	USABLE FUEL			
	GALLONS	POUNDS JP-5	POUNDS JP-4	
Number 1	418	2,840	2,720	
Number 2 Left Engine Feed	263	1,790	1,710	
Number 3 Right Engine Feed	206	1,400	1,340	
Number 4	532	3,620	3,460	
Total Fuselage	1,419	9,650	9,230	
Left and Right Internal Wings	85 / 85 / 170	580 / 580 / 1,160	550 / 550 / 1,100	
Total Internal	1,589	10,810	10,330	

EXTERNAL TANK(S)			
Elliptical Wing or Centerline Tank	314	2,140	2,040
Cylindrical Wing or Centerline Tank	330	2,240	2,150

NOTES

- The fuel quantities, in pounds, are rounded off to the nearest 10 pounds. Therefore, the actual gallons times 6.8 or 6.5 will not necessarily agree with the pounds column.
- Fuel weights are based on JP-5 or JP-4 at 6.8 or 6.5 pounds per gallon and a temperature of 15°C (59°F).

F/A-18A

F/A-18C

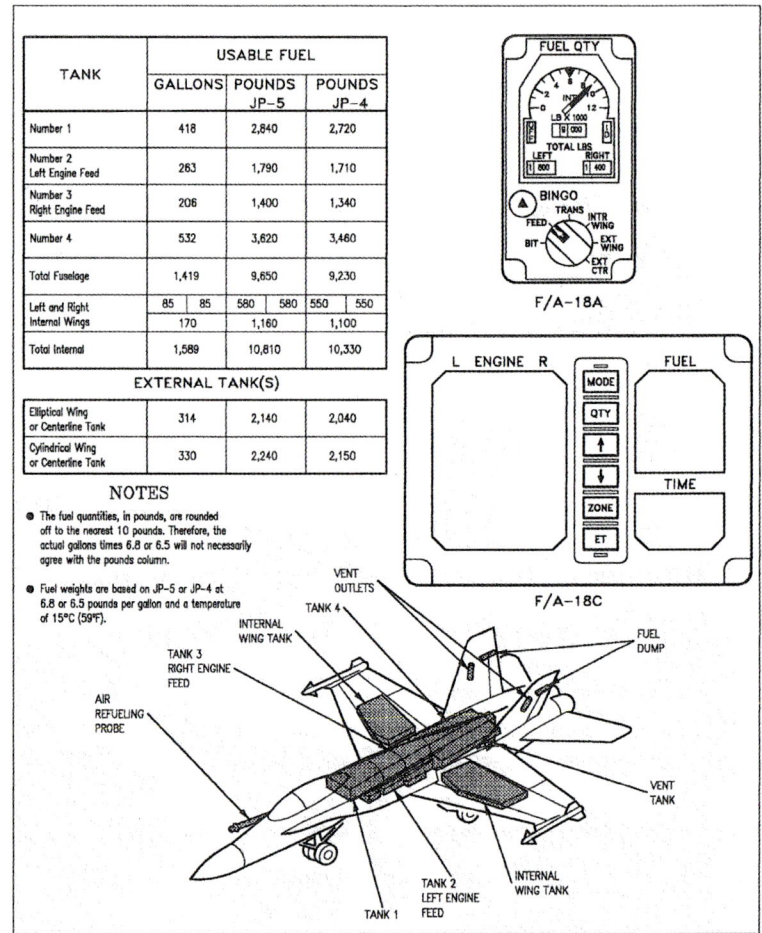

Figure 2-6. Fuel Quantity (F/A-18A/C)

I-2-23   ORIGINAL

The general dimensions of the F/A-18 are shown here. *US Navy*

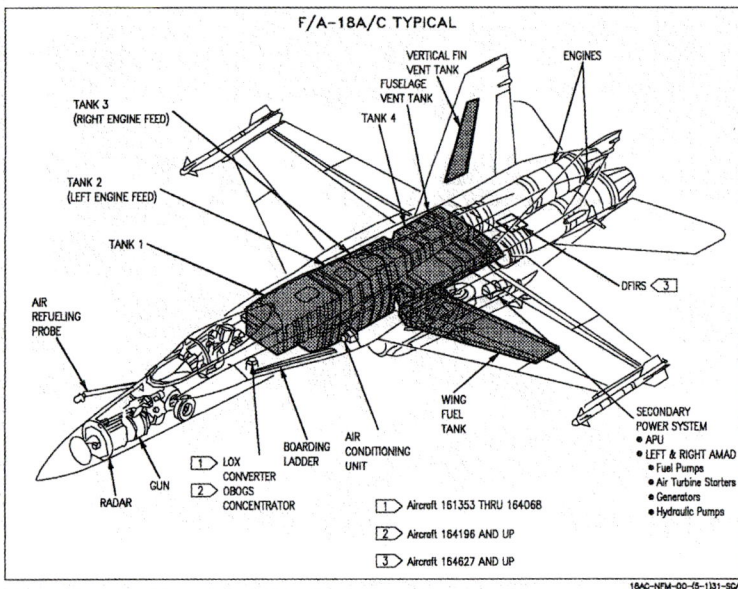

Figure 1-1. General Arrangement (F/A-18A/C)

1.1.4 Mission. The aircraft has an all-weather intercept, identify, destroy, and ground attack capability. Air-to-air armament normally consists of AIM-9, AIM-7, and AIM-120 missiles and a 20 mm gun. Various air-to-ground stores may be carried. Mission range may be extended with the addition of up to three external fuel tanks.

This general arrangement illustration from an F/A-18A/C NATOPS shows the primary structural components of the F/A-18. The wings and forward fuselage sections were manufactured at the McDonnell Douglas (now Boeing) facility in St. Louis while the aft fuselage was manufactured at Northrop's El Segundo facility. *US Navy*

Although the YF-17 was optimized as a fighter, the Navy required the derivative to be capable in the air-to-ground mode so as to replace the F-4 Phantom II, A-4 Skyhawk, and A-7 Corsair II. This image of TF-1 touts the Hornet's significant air-to-ground capability, with weapons ranging from standard Mk.80 series iron bombs to Zuni rocket pods to cluster bomb munitions. *Boeing via Tony Landis*

The Hornet made its first flight on November 18, 1978, flying from McDonnell Douglas' St. Louis facility to Springfield, Illinois, and back. FSD No.1 (BuNo. 160775) carried a crisp white, blue, and gold paint scheme and featured "Navy" on the right side of the fuselage under the LEX and "Marines" on the left. *Boeing*

Although Northrop developed the YF-17, the "navalization" of the aircraft led to McDonnell Douglas becoming primary contractor. Northrop continued to manufacture the Hornet's center and aft fuselage section, including the twin vertical stabilizers, and assorted subsystems, which is transported to St. Louis from California via a flat truck bed. Here, Northrop delivers the 800th Hornet strike fighter shipset. *Northrop Grumman*

An innovation of the F/A-18 was provisioning for the fuselage carriage of two AIM-7 Sparrow missiles. The Sparrow (and now AIM-120 AMRAAM) gave the Hornet a medium-range air-to-air missile capability. *US Navy via Museum of Naval Aviation*

The Hornet's cockpit represented a significant step forward from even the new F-14 and F-15, which still relied on gauges and dials. Shown here are three multi-functional displays that permit the pilot to access all information concerning aircraft mission and weapons systems, as well as the radar. This image shows the cockpit of an F/A-18C circa 1994. The main difference from the A model is the presence of the digital/CRT display fuel monitor and engine monitor. *Brad Elward*

The Hands-On-Throttle-And-Stick (HOTAS) controls place all of the key functions at the pilot's disposal without the need to look back into the cockpit. *Paul Carlson*

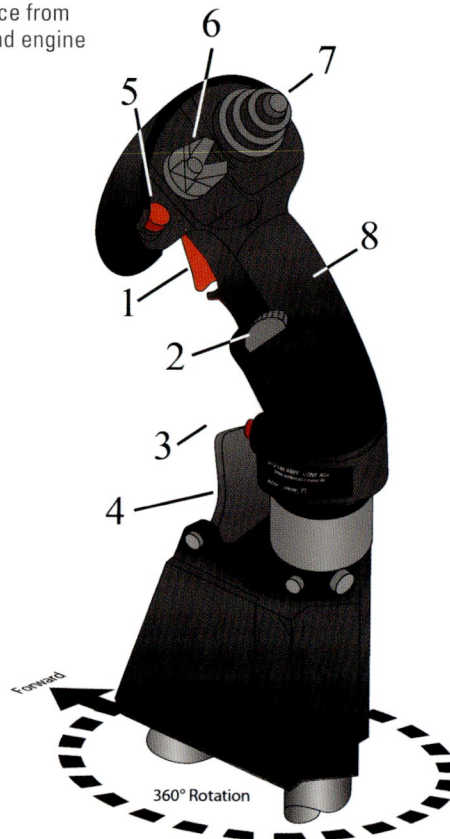

THROTTLE
1 Communications Selector
2 Dispense Switch
3 Throttle Designator Controller
4 ATC Engage/Disengage
5 RAID/FLIR FOV Select Button
6 Exterior Lights
7 Radar Antenna Elevation
8 Throttle Control Slider
9 Speed Brake Control

STICK
1 Trigger Switch
2 Weapons Selector
3 Undesignate Nosewheel Steering
4 Nosewheel Steering Disengage
  Auto Pilot Disengage
  G Limiter Override Switch
5 Air/Ground Weapon Release Button
6 Sensor Control Switch
7 Pitch and Roll Trim Switch
8 Pitch and Roll Control Handle

THROTTLE

STICK

FSD No.6 (BuNo. 160780) was the first to be painted in the red on white color scheme and was used for high angle-of-attack and spin testing. After delivery to Pax River, the aircraft was fitted with an explosively-deployed anti-spin chute. F6 first flew on August 27, 1979. *Don Linn*

FSD No.2 (BuNo. 160776) undergoes shipboard barricade testing at NAEC Lakehurst on September 6, 1983. *US Navy via Robert F. Dorr*

Seen here at NAS Patuxent River in October 1982, FSD No.3 (BuNo. 160777) is fitted with an AIM-7 mock-up on its fuselage station. No.3 was used largely for carrier suitability testing and environmental control system testing. *Don Linn*

The Hornet underwent its initial carrier qualifications aboard USS *America* (CV-66) from October 30, to November 3, 1979. The tests, flown by LCDR Dick Richards and LT Ken Grubbs, involved thirty-two catapult launches and traps, and seventeen touch and go landings. *Boeing*

A key feature of the Hornet's ease of maintenance is its easily accessible panels, which allows ground crews to access critical aircraft and mission system electronics from ground level. *US Navy*

The "D" shaped inlet for the F404-GE-400 engine is shown in this image, along with the splitter plate between the inlet and the Hornet's fuselage, which allows boundary air to bleed away from the aircraft and also into the aircraft's ECS intake. Also note the angled SUU-62 centerline pylon holding the 330-gallon (1249.1 l) fuel tank. The original SUU-62, used through Lot 10, featured a flat or straight leading edge design versus the angled aft version shown here. *Ted Carlson*

The Hornet's engines can be easily removed and replaced and are considered "neutral," meaning that a single engine would fit into either side of the fuselage. The interior of the engine well is coated with a heat-resistant white paint to help highlight any fluid leaks. *US Navy*

FSD No.4 (BuNo. 160778) is shown here dropping a load of nine 1,000-lb. (453.5 kg) Mk.83 bombs during flight testing. Two bombs each were carried on the wing stations and a single bomb was carried on the centerline station. FSD Nos. 5 (160779), 7 (160782), and T1 (160781) were also involved in the weapons testing program. *Boeing via Dennis Jenkins*

F-5 was heavily involved in armament systems testing and was the first to conduct a live missile firing. In December 1979, FSD No.5 fired an AIM-9 Sidewinder heat-seeking missile and scored a near-miss on a BQM-34 target (the warhead was not live). The image here shows an AIM-7 Sparrow and a wing-tip AIM-9 Sidewinder. *US Navy via Naval Aviation Museum*

An F/A-18B from NAS Patuxent River launches an AGM-88 High-speed Anti-Radiation Missile (HARM) during a test-firing verifying a trouble-free separation from the aircraft. Notice the Mk.83 bomb on the right wing. *Texas Instruments*

The Hornet includes the six-barrel M61A1 Vulcan cannon, which fires 20 mm high-explosive, armor-piercing incendiary, or inert target practice rounds at 4,000 or 6,000 rounds per minute. The lighter M61A2 was used on BuNo. 164725 (Lot 15) and up. The Hornet carriers 578 rounds fully loaded. *US Navy*

FSD No.4 carries a pair of AIM-7 Sparrow missiles on its fuselage (stations 4 and 6) and wingtip-mounted AIM-9 Sidewinder missiles (stations 1 and 9). *Boeing*

The APG-65, developed by Hughes (later Raytheon), was a remarkably easy to maintain radar that was the first to combine an effective air-to-air and air-to-ground capability into a single unit. The radar could easily transition between modes by a click of a switch, making possible the strike fighter mission. *US Navy*

The YF-17 was flown and evaluated by instructors at the Navy's Fighter Weapons School (TOPGUN) in the late 1970s. *US Navy*

The final FSD aircraft (BuNo. 160785) was manufactured to near-production standards. FSD No.8 is painted in a low-visibility gray paint scheme common for Navy tactical aircraft. *US Navy*

Shown here with four 1,000 lb. (453.5 kg) Mk.83 bombs, two wingtip AIM-9 Sidewinders, three 315-gallon elliptical fuel tanks, an AAQ-38 FLIR pod, and a Martin Marietta ASQ-173 laser spot tracker/strike camera (LST/SCAM). This configuration was flown at the request of then-Navy Secretary John Lehman to demonstrate once and for all that the Hornet was capable of performing its mission with ample range. BuNo. 161248 flew from NAS Patuxent River to Florida's Pinecastle Range Complex near Jacksonville and back, and the test was deemed a success. *Boeing*

VX-4 conducted the fighter portion of the Hornet's operational evaluation (OpEval) and gave its approval of the aircraft, finding it operationally capable and operationally effective. Because of the Hornet's unique strike fighter mission, a separate OpEval was also conducted by VX-5 to evaluate the aircraft's performance in the attack mission. Shown here is a VX-4 Hornet on USS *Carl Vinson* (CVN-70) circa 1984. *Don Linn*

VX-4's fighter OpEval was deemed a success, but focused solely on the Hornet's air-to-air mission, which included fighter sweep, intercept, and escort missions. The early model F/A-18A shown here carries two AIM-7 (fuselage) and two AIM-9 (wingtip) missiles. *Lou Drendel*

As the testing phase completed, Hornets were assigned to train the instructors for the Fleet Introduction Team (FIT) and Fleet Replacement Squadron (FRS). Here a TF-18 (later designated as F/A-18B) from VFA-125 *Rough Raiders*, the first F/A-18 FRS, is shown aboard USS *Carl Vinson* (CVN-70) in 1984. VFA-125, based at NAS Lemoore, trained the initial fleet squadrons as well as helped establish VFA-106 *Gladiators*, the East Coast Navy FRS, and VMFAT-101 *Sharpshooters*, the sole Marine Corps FRS. *Don Linn*

A fully-loaded F/A-18 sits ready on the runway. This Hornet carriers two wingtip-mounted AIM-9 Sidewinders for air-to-air defense, sensor pods on stations 4 and 6, and at least fourteen 500-lb. (226.7 kg) Mk.82 high-drag (retarded) bombs on both wing stations and the centerline station. *Boeing*

Almost all Hornet developmental testing was conducted at NAS Patuxent River, Maryland, under a new Principal Site Concept, where the bulk of flight test work was done at a central location rather than scattered around the country or split between the Navy and manufacturer, as had prior programs. By mid-1981, the program had accumulated more than 3,500 flight hours and more than 2,600 flights. Here FSD No.4 readies for a mission with four Mk.82 iron bombs and two fuel tanks. Notice the tanks have now transitioned to the oval 330-gallon tanks from the initial elliptical 315-gallon tanks. The latter created excessive drag and were prone to fatigue cracks. *Don Linn*

A Canadian CF-188A reveals its clean lines and notable leading-edge flaps. *Neil Pearson*

A US Navy F/A-18D from VFA-106 readies for flight. Notice the folded wings, which enable easier carrier storage. The ailerons are located on the outer portion of the wing from the wingfold mechanism outward. The Hornet's trailing-edge flaps run from the wingfold inwards and can droop forty-five degrees for landing. *Neil Pearson*

CHAPTER 3

F/A-18A/B

VFA-125 *Rough Raiders* was commissioned in 1980, and received its first Hornet (BuNo. 161214/F-11) in February 1981, an F/A-18A from VX-4. The squadron received its first two-seat trainer (BuNo. 161217/T3) the following month from McDonnell Douglas. In March 1981, nine squadron pilots began transitioning to the F/A-18. *Don Linn*

While retaining many core YF-17 features, such as the dual engines, the LEX, and the twin canted stabilizers, the redesigned F-18 (Model 267) did not share a single dimension with the YF-17. The aft fuselage area was widened four inches, enlarging the fuselage spine, and the engines were toed slightly outward. A retractable hose and drogue-capable refueling probe was added and internal fuel capacity was increased to 10,800 lbs. (4,898.8 kg).

The Hornet received the new 15,800-lb. thrust (70.45 kN) F404-GE-400 turbofan engines, which were designed as "neutral" power plants, meaning that the same engine fits in either engine bay. The aircraft's wing area grew from 350 to 400 square feet (from 32.5 to 37.2 square meters) and the wing span was increased by two feet (6.09 cm). Wing chord was also increased, and the leading and trailing edge flaps were redesigned and reprogrammed to improve low speed handling characteristics.

To remedy an anticipated flutter problem discovered during the F-15 flight tests, a small wing "snag" or "dogtooth" discontinuity was added on the leading edge of both the wing flaps and the stabilators. The aircraft's stabilators were also enlarged and given a lower aspect ratio. Similar to the YF-17, the F-18's twin vertical stabilizers were canted outward, but at a twenty- rather than eighteen-degree angle. All control surfaces were computer-controlled by a quadruple redundant fly-by-wire system for optimal performance during all flight regimes. The F-18 utilized five control surfaces: ailerons, leading- and trailing-edge flaps, stabilators, and rudders. Directional control was provided by the rudders, with roll control provided by differential movements of the stabilators, ailerons, and leading- and trailing-edge flaps. Pitch control was obtained by moving the stabilators together.

The F-18 featured nine external stores stations. The two wingtip stations carry the AIM-9 Sidewinder missile, while two wing stations, rated at 2,500 lbs. (1,134 kg) and 2,350 lbs. (1.065.9 kg)

from inboard to outboard, are located under each wing for air-to-air or air-to-ground munitions. The inboard stations can also carry fuel tanks, originally the 315-gallon (1,192.4 liter) elliptical tank and later the 330-gallon (1,249.1 l) tank. The centerline station, rated at 2,600 lbs. (1,174.3 kg), was available for air-to-ground weapons or a fuel tank. One of the innovations of the F-18 program was the conversion of the two fuselage stations into dual weapons and sensor stations. When the aircraft was originally conceived in two variants, the fighter version (F-18) was to carry the AIM-7 Sparrow on the fuselage stations, while the attack variant (A-18) was to carry the Ford Aerospace AAS-38 NITE Hawk FLIR on the right station and the Martin Marietta ASQ-173 LDT/SCAM pod on the left station.

Radar Improvements Combines the F-18/A-18 Mission into One Airframe

Because the YF-17 was designed as an air-to-air fighter, its Westinghouse radar offered limited range and could not control radar-guided weapons. Yet Navy officials insisted on a Sparrow missile capability, causing McDonnell Douglas to turn to the Hughes (now Raytheon) APG-65 digital multi-mode pulse-Doppler J-band "look-down, shoot-down" radar. The Hughes radar required an enlarged nose radome diameter to accommodate the larger twenty-eight-inch (71.92 cm) antenna. The cockpit was also moved back four inches.

Designing a radar compact enough for the limited space allotted in the Hornet (only 4.45 cubic feet) proved most challenging. Unlike the large and powerful AWG-9 radar, around which the F-14 was designed, the Hornet's radar had to be specifically designed to fit into the smaller airframe. The one disadvantage, however, was the APG-65's reduced power, which meant a considerably reduced comparative detection range versus the

F-15's APG-63. Hughes succeeded in producing a compact design (less than forty percent of the APG-63's weight), that could perform well in both the air-to-air and air-to-ground mode. This proved a key point in the F/A-18's evolution, allowing a single aircraft to perform both the fighter and attack mission without the need to change any systems; the pilot need only flip a switch. The radar has proven to be reliable and easy to maintain.

The F-18 and A-18 had been sold on the idea that two similar airframes would reduce costs by leading to an economy of scale for parts and maintainers; moreover, with the change of a few black boxes, an F-18 could become an A-18 and vice versa. Now these economies were even more significant because no reconfiguration was needed. The F-18 and A-18 designations were abandoned in 1980, in favor of the F/A-18, signaling the birth of the true modern-day strike-fighter.

Glass Cockpit Design

The F-18's revolutionary cockpit ushered in the so-called "glass cockpit" design now standard on military and most commercial aircraft. A key feature was the tactical Heads-Up Display or HUD; a small glass screen on top of the cockpit that displays critical flight and weapon information. A pilot looking through the HUD sees "symbology" representing information needed to fly the plane in combat without the need to look back into the cockpit. While the HUD was not a new concept, the Hornet was the first tactical aircraft to use it as a principal flight instrument. Another significant part of the cockpit was the "hands-on-throttle-and-stick" system, called HOTAS, which allows a pilot to control all sensors and weapons needed for air combat, thereby dispensing with the need to look inside the cockpit during critical moments.

The Hornet's cockpit featured three five-by-five inch (12.7-by-12.7 cm) Multi-Functional Displays (MFDs) which presented pilots with computerized menus allowing them to access literally dozens of "pages" of information ranging from threat data to systems checks to radar information. The information can be accessed by pressing a button along the side of the screen and moving progressively deeper into the "book." Both the left and right displays can present the same information in the event of a failure. The center display offered a color moving map. A limited number of back-up gauges and instruments are at the lower right in the event of a computer failure.

The Two-Place F/A-18B

The TF-18 was initially designed as a two-place training aircraft with dual pilot controls fitted in the aft cockpit. To accommodate the second cockpit, the forward-most fuel bladder was removed, reducing the overall fuel capacity by six percent. The aft cockpit featured a separate stick and throttle, but lacked a HUD and a tail hook control. F/A-18Bs were used almost exclusively by the three FRS squadrons to train new Hornet pilots and by VAQ-34, the Navy's now disestablished electronic aggressor squadron. Interestingly, the Marines and not the Navy recognized the F/A-18B's potential as a tactical aircraft and adopted the B and later the F/A-18D in that role to replace the A-6Es.

Operational History

VFA-125 *Rough Raiders*, the F/A-18 Fleet Readiness Squadron (FRS) and first Hornet squadron, received its first F/A-18s at NAS Lemoore, California, on November 13, 1980, and immediately began training the instructors who would, in turn, train Hornet fleet units. The squadron spent much of the following year developing and preparing the new training syllabus. Because VFA-125 was to train both the Navy and Marine Corps Hornet pilots and maintainers, it was manned from the start as a joint service squadron, with equal numbers of men from each service on the staff.

On January 7, 1983, the first Hornet squadron, VMFA-314 *Black Knights* at MCAS El Toro, California, was declared operational; VMFAs-323 *Death Rattlers* and -531 *Grey Ghosts* followed shortly thereafter. The first Navy squadrons to receive the F/A-18A were VFAs-25 *Fist of the Fleet* and -113 *Stingers* of Air Wing 14. These two Navy squadrons later made the Hornets' first operational deployment aboard *Constellation* during 1985. A second FRS, VFA-106 *Gladiators*, stood up at NAS Cecil Field, the East Coast F/A-18 base, on April 27, 1984. Interestingly, the first three East Coast F/A-18 squadrons, VFAs-131 *Wildcats*, -132 *Privateers*, and -136 *Knight Hawks*, were all commissioned at Lemoore, and then transferred to Cecil Field. A third Hornet FRS, VMFAT-101 *Sharp Shooters*, was established at MCAS El Toro in 1988 to train Marine pilots, Weapons Systems Operators (WSOs), and maintainers.

A total of 371 F/A-18As and thirty-nine F/A-18Bs were built for the US Navy and Marine Corps through mid-1987, with the last F/A-18A (163175) delivered to VMFA-312 on January 22, 1988. In 2003, F/A-18A was completely withdrawn from Navy service, with VFA-97 *Warhawks* taking the type into its final combat during Iraqi Freedom. The F/A-18A+ is still in service with two Marine Corps reserve squadrons. The F/A-18A/B has also been flown by Navy and Marine Corps Reserve squadrons, various test squadrons, TOPGUN, Strike, and NASA, whose work has concentrated on testing high angle-of-attack vehicles (HARV) and thrust-vectored engines. The *Blue Angels*, the Navy's Flight Demonstration Team, adopted the F/A-18A in February 1987, replacing the A-4F Skyhawk flown since 1974.

The first operational Hornet squadron was Marine Corps' VMFA-1314 *Black Knights*, which transitioned from the F-4 Phantom II. The squadron joined Carrier Air Wing 13 (CVW-13) in 1985 and participated in Operation *El Dorado Canyon* in 1986 in the Gulf of Sidra, and later flew 814 combat sorties in support of Operation *Desert Storm*, more than any other Navy or Marine Corps squadron. *Don Linn*

Two USMC F/A-18Ds highlight the Hornets ability to fly with a variety of stores, including asymmetrical loads. While both aircraft carry two external fuel tanks and two GPS-guided GBU-32(v) 1,000-lb (450 kg) JDAM bombs, the Hornet in the foreground has a centerline and inner port wing tank, and the Hornet in the background has tanks mounted on the inner wing pylons. *Jamie Hunter*

The second Navy fleet squadron to fly the Hornet, VFA-25 *Fist of the Fleet* began its transition as part of Class 9-83 in July 1983. The *Fisties* would later be paired with VFA-113 *Stingers* aboard CVW-14. Here, an F/A-18A practices carrier landings aboard USS *Constellation* (CV-64) in the Southern California Operating Area in 1984. *US Navy*

VFA-113 *Stingers* was the Navy's first operational fleet squadron to fly the Hornet. After trading in their A-7E Corsair II light attack aircraft, the *Stingers* began their transition in March 1983 as part of Class 6-83. The squadron traded in their Alpha models for F/A-18C, shown here, in 1989. *US Navy*

The AIM-7 Sparrow, shown here on an F/A-18C, was the primary medium range weapon for the Hornet until the AIM-120 AMRAAM was introduced in the late 1980s. The Sparrow was a semi-active radar homing missile, which required the pilot to keep the Hornet pointed at the target aircraft to illuminate it until the missile detonated. This meant the pilot could not maneuver to avoid enemy missiles or aircraft, or else risk breaking radar lock. *US Navy via Dennis Jenkins*

The F/A-18 initially carried two banks of Tracor ALE-39 chaff/flare/jammer countermeasures dispenser, each containing thirty cartridges. Later Hornet models beginning with the Lot 18 F/A-18C in the late 1990s received the more advanced ALE-47 countermeasures system, shown here. Both are located under the intake duct. Some Hornets received two additional sets of dispensers. *Ted Carlson*

An effective weapon for air-to-ground attack (close air support) is the LAU-10 rocket launcher with 5˝ Zuni rockets. The pod holds four rockets and the Hornet can carry up to eight pods. The dual pods here are mounted on a BSU-33/A Vertical Ejector Rack (VER) to the outer wing pylon. *Ted Carlson*

The AGM-62 Walleye and Walleye II were occasionally seen on F/A-18s. The Walleye was a television-guided glide bomb dating back to the 1960s, and featured an 825-lb. (374 kg) high-explosive warhead. Walleyes were largely replaced by the AGM-65 Maverick, although some were used during the 1991 Gulf War. The glide bomb was guided using the AWW-9 (and later AWW-13) two-way datalink carried by the launching aircraft or its wingman. *US Navy*

The first three East Coast Hornet squadrons were trained at NAS Lemoore by VFA-125 and then relocated to NAS Cecil Field, Florida, where they stayed until 1999 before moving to NAS Oceana in Virginia. Shown here are aircraft from the East Coast FRS, VFA-106 *Gladiators*, and two fleet squadrons, VFA-131 *Wildcats* and VFA-132 *Privateers*. The *Privateers* were short-lived and disestablished in 1992 due to the post-Cold War drawdown, but VFA-131 is still flying the F/A-18C as of publication. *Don Linn*

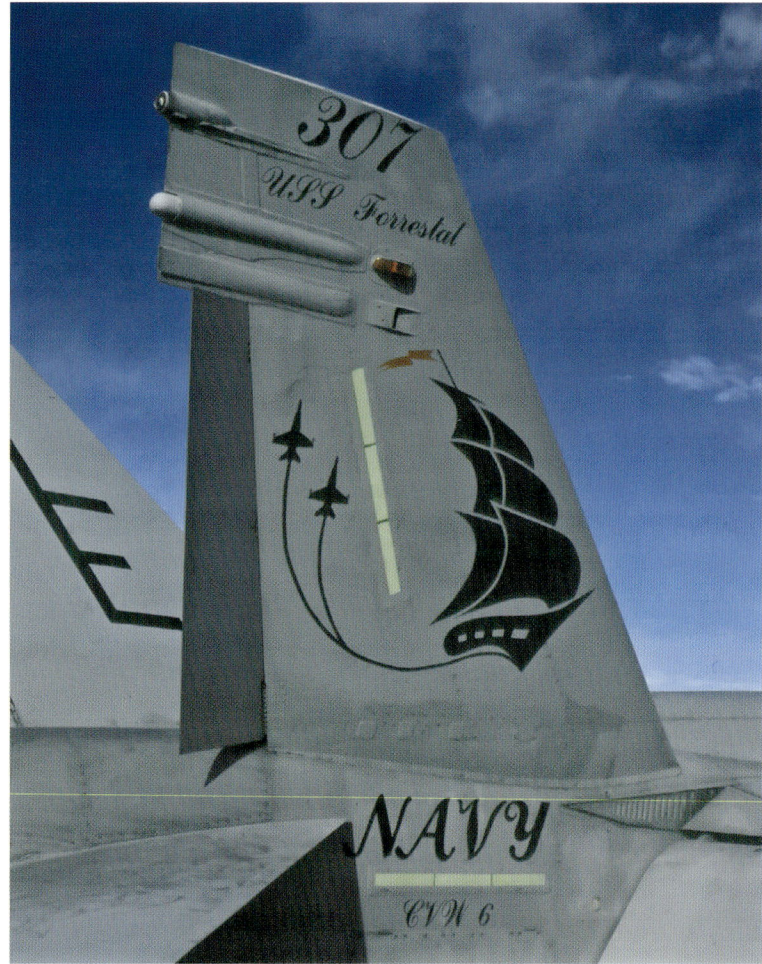

The F/A-18A's right tailfin shows from top to bottom, a white navigation light, ALR-67 RWR antenna, and a fuel dump vent. The small opening ahead of the fuel dump is the fuel vent pressurization air intake and above that is a red anti-collision light. The left tailfin is identical except the top fixture is replaced with an electronic countermeasures (ECM) antennae. The A's tailfin differs from that of the C model, which adds a high-band ALQ-165 antenna on top, a new middle ALR-67 RWR antenna, and adds a new low-band ALQ-165 antenna on the bottom (see page 79). *David Brown*

Note the clean lines of the LEX on this VFA-131 F/A-18A Hornet, circa 1985. *Don Linn*

The two-seat F/A-18B, previously referred to as the TF-18, was used primarily for pilot training at the FRS level, although some could be found at the adversary and fleet composite squadrons, as well as Test Pilot School and the VX test and evaluation squadrons. This F/A-18B from VMFAT-101, the Marine Corps F/A-18 FRS now based at MCAS Miramar, appears in a two-tone blue camouflage scheme. *Bill Shemley*

The LEX fences were added in May 1988 to help redirect the vortices created by the LEX, which were adding unforeseen stress and fatigue to the Hornet's vertical stabilizers and resulting in premature cracking. The fatigue problems became so severe that the F/A-18 fleet was grounded pending a resolution. The fix was installation of a LEX fence to prevent generation of the vortices. *Ted Carlson*

The Navy Test Pilot School flies several A and B model F/A-18s. *US Navy*

The F/A-18A quickly entered service with the US Navy and Marine Corps Reserve squadrons, beginning with VFAs-303 *Golden Hawks* and -305 *Lobos* in 1984 and 1987, and VFMA-134 *Hawks* in 1983. The *Blue Dolphins* of VFA-204 were based in Jacksonville, Florida, and Atlanta, Georgia, and flew the Hornet from 1989 to 2004. During that time the squadron stood ready to deploy as an activated carrier-based reserve squadron, but also served as adversaries for fleet fighter and strike fighter squadrons preparing to deploy. *US Navy*

The Hornet's engine nozzles feature twelve petals that open and close depending on the thrust desired. Notice the edge of the pedal flaps, referred to as "shingled flaps," which appear on all production Hornets after 1987 and all remaining Hornet post-1995. Prior to 1987, all Hornets featured straight outer edge flaps. The tail hook, located between the engines, is inspected after every ten arrested landings and the tip is replaced after 120 arrested landings. The entire hook is replaced after 1,200 arrested landings. *Brad Elward*

The Hornet uses a single point refueling system located on the aircraft's port side. Fuel is carried in four interconnected fuselage tanks and two internal wing (wet) tanks and can be carried in external fuel tanks mounted on the inner wing or centerline pylons. The single-seat Hornet carries up to 10,810 lbs. (4,903.3 kg) of usable JP-5 fuel (1,589 gallons/6,015 l) and each 330-gallon (1,249 l) external tank holds 2,240 lbs. (1,016 kg). *US Navy*

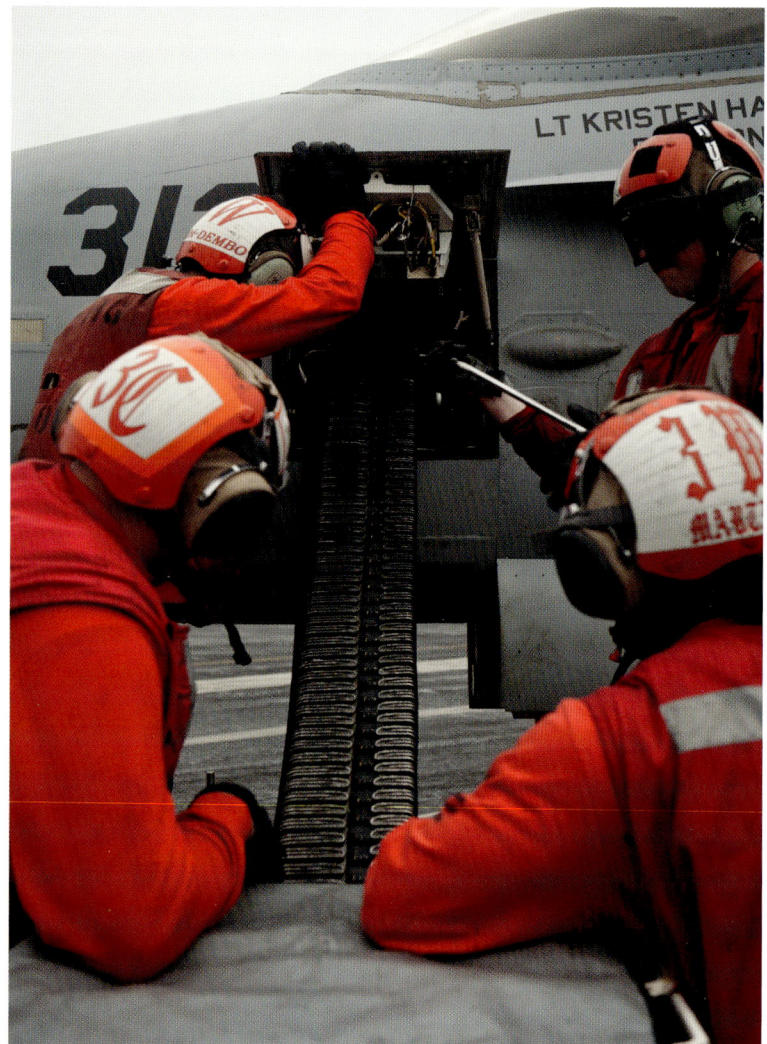

This image shows maintenance personnel working on the Hornet's gun aboard a carrier. The large barrel contains the ammunition, which is then fed via a belt into the gun cannon. Although ammo capacity is stated at 578 rounds, Hornets at sea typically carry only 500 rounds, as all rounds are required to be inside the ammo drum when the aircraft is aboard the carrier. A gun can be removed and replaced in less than two hours. *US Navy*

F/A-18A Hornets from VFAs-25 and -113, the Navy's first operational Hornet squadrons, are shown flying in formation as they return from the USS *Independence* (CV-62) in December 1990. At the time, the carrier was returning from the Persian Gulf following its participation in Operation *Desert Shield*. The carrier and its air wing had been on station in the Gulf when Iraq invaded Kuwait in August 1990. *US Navy*

As the more capable F/A-18C began entering fleet service, F/A-18A aircraft were assigned to support additional reserve squadrons. Here, a line of F/A-18As belonging to VFA-127 *Desert Bogies* can be seen at NAS Fallon. The squadron, which operated Hornets from 1992-1996, provided adversary support for Navy fleet squadrons. The four aircraft at the end of the line are F-5E Tigers.
US Navy via Naval Aviation Museum

VFA-86 *Sidewinders* transitioned to the F/A-18C Hornet beginning in July 1987. The *Sidewinders* were the first East Coast squadron to receive the new F/A-18C. The squadron was based at NAS Cecil Field until the based closed in 1999, and was one of two Navy Hornet squadrons that moved to MCAS Beaufort, South Carolina, rather than NAS Oceana. This image highlights the dark Kevlar coating applied to the walkway along the cockpit and fuselage spine. VFA-86 was operating with CVW-1 aboard USS *America* (CV-66) at the time of this photo. The squadron now flies the F/A-18E Super Hornet. *US Navy via Jim Sullivan*

The Hornet features a Hands-On Throttle and Stick (HOTAS) control system that permits the pilot to control all significant flight and weapons systems. The dual throttle control has nine switches while the stick, which controls flight direction, contains eight switches. These are used in conjunction with the Heads-Up Display (HUD) cues to help the pilot operate the jet without looking down into the cockpit.
Ted Carlson

The F/A-18 cockpit is shown in these three images. The throttle is located on the pilot's left and the stick is located in the center between the pilot's legs. The HUD shows flight speed, direction, altitude, and various weapons symbols and cues. *Ted Carlson*

The Hornet was originally equipped with the SJU-5/A and -6/A ejection seat (Lot 12 and below). These were replaced with the Naval Aircrew Common Ejection Seat (NACES) SJU-17(V)1/A, 2/A, and 9/A, and SJU-17A(V)1/A, 2/A, and 9/A after Lot 13, and also fitted into F/A-18A+ aircraft after AFC 493. Safe escape is provided for most combinations of aircraft altitude, speed, attitude, and flight path within the envelope of 0 to 600 KIAS airspeed, and 0 to 50,000-ft. altitude. *Ted Carlson*

Two F/A-18As from VFC-12 *Fighting Omars*. The squadron transitioned to the F/A-18A/B in 1994 then traded these aircraft for F/A-18A+ in 2004. The squadron traded these jets with VFA-87 for F/A-18Cs in 2006, and switched them back in 2012. VFC-12 provides support for the Strike Fighter Advanced Readiness Program (SFARP), which involves an intense three-week training program administered by the Strike Fighter Weapons School, Atlantic. The *Fighting Omars* also support VFA-106 training at both NAS Oceana and through detachments to NAS Key West. *Ted Carlson*

Six VFC-12 aircraft are seen here making a series of quick break turns. All feature a single centerline tank and have no pylons affixed to their wings. A Hornet in this configuration is extremely maneuverable.
Ted Carlson

An F/A-18B from VFC-12 makes an arrested landing aboard USS *Ronald Reagan* (CVN-76) in 2005. Note the two-tone grey paint scheme. *US Navy*

An F/A-18C from VX-23 is on final approach behind the USS *Ronald Reagan* (CVN-76). The individuals on the platform are Landing Signal Officers (LSOs), who help the pilot in the final stages of the approach. An LSO is usually present for each squadron that will be landing as well as an air wing or CAG LSO. The Hornet is one of the best handling aircraft behind the carrier. *US Navy*

Hornets were also operated by VFC-13 *Saints* from 1992 to 1993 when the squadron was based at NAS Miramar. The squadron was relocated to NAS Fallon in 1996, just ahead of TOPGUN's relocation to Fallon, and at that time transitioned to the F-5E, F-5F, and F-5N. *David Brown*

The F-18 Hornet has served with the *Blue Angels* since 1987. The *Blue Angels* typically operate ten–eleven aircraft, although they fly six in any given show. At least two of the *Blue Angels* aircraft are two-seat F/A-18B or F/A-18D models, which are used for VIP rides. *US Navy*

The *Blue Angels* aircraft are modified by Boeing to remove the gun and tactical equipment; a smoke generator and ILS are also added, as well as internal provisions to permit sustained inverted flight. The *Blue Angels* will replace their Hornets with Super Hornets beginning with the 2017 season. *Neil Pearson*

An F/A-18A Hornet from VMFA-323 launches an AIM-7 Sparrow missile in July 1986. The *Death Rattlers* are based at MCAS Miramar and are under the command of Marine Aircraft Group (MAG) 11 and the 3rd Marine Aircraft Wing (3rd MAW), but deploy with CVW-11. The squadron transitioned to the F/A-18A from the F-4 Phantom II in 1982 and deployed aboard USS *Coral Sea* (CV-43) during the *El Dorado Canyon* raids. The squadron made several Southern Watch deployments and has deployed during *Iraqi Freedom. US Navy*

NASA operates several F/A-18As for a variety of test evaluations and as chase aircraft. *Lou Drendel*

VFA-125 trains F/A-18 pilots (and aircraft maintainers) and has a structured program that includes multi-phased instruction. Part of the student training syllabus includes a Carrier Qualifications (CQ) Phase, which is the first time students take the Hornet to the carrier. This photo depicts a *Rough Raiders'* F/A-18A Hornet moving up to the catapult on USS *Carl Vinson* (CVN-70) in January 1986. *US Navy*

Boeing (then McDonnell Douglas) experimented with a reconnaissance version of the Hornet in 1984 and prepared two prototypes for evaluation. Shown here is BuNo. 160775 modified to accept an internal sensor package in place of its 20 mm cannon. It first flew August 15, 1984. The second aircraft modified for recce study was BuNo. 161214. *Boeing*

The Northrop production line produced the center and aft fuselage section of the aircraft, including the vertical stabilizers. *Northrop via Tony Landis*

The two-seat F/A-18B was flown by VAQ-34 *Flashbacks*, a Tactical Electronic Warfare Squadron, out of the Pacific Missile Test Center, Point Mugu, California, and later NAS Lemoore. The *Flashbacks* provided electronic support for fleet exercises and simulated a variety of electronic threats. The squadron disestablished in 1993. *US Navy*

A blue camouflaged VFC-13 F/A-18A flies in formation with a sharply painted VFA-204 River Rattler. *Ted Carlson*

An excellent close-up of an F/A-18A from VFA-97 *Warhawks* seen in October 1993. This was one of the last fleet squadrons to fly the F/A-18A. Notice the lack of APX-111X antennas across the nose and the AAS-38 Nite Hawk FLIR on the fuselage station 4. *US Navy*

An F/A-18A (BuNo. 161710) from VMFA-314 flies near Point Mugu in March 1983. *Don Linn*

By the mid-1980s, operational use had revealed what the Hornet was capable of, and further highlighted areas that needed improvement. Fortunately, the Hornet airframe structure offered ample room for growth, both in avionics and in systems space, which allowed designers to continually add new and improved avionics components, upgraded software, and weaponry. As the 1980s progressed, designers sought to further develop the Hornet by adding an all-weather attack capability, the AIM-120 AMRAAM missile, and improved survivability. What followed became the ultimate development in the Legacy Hornet line—the F/A-18C/D Night Attack Hornet—and one through which the aircraft's true capability emerged.

The F/A-18C began as an Engineering Change Proposal (ECP-178) to the F/A-18A to incorporate the ALQ-165 Airborne Self-Protection Jammer (ASPJ), a new data link (JTDS), and AGM-65E laser Maverick, as well as other performance enhancements. F/A-18C/D added a substantially upgraded Stores Management System and armament system, a new flight incident recorder system, and XN-6 mission computer. The latter introduced a three-fold increase in processing speed and twice the memory of the F/A-18A's XN-5. Externally, a host of new ECM antennas were added and ALQ-67 radar warning receiver antennas were added to the fuselage under the nose in a unique five stub pattern. Lot 10 introduced the AMRAAM capability; the Martin-Baker NACES ejection seat was added with production Lot 13, Block 33 (F/A-18D 164196).

An F/A-18A (163427) modified to "C" standards flew on September 3, 1987. VFA-86 *Sidewinders*, the first East Coast Charlie squadron, obtained their Hornets in 1987; VFAs-25 and -113 became the first West Coast Charlie squadrons in June 1989. Boeing built 137 F/A-18Cs before starting production of the more capable night attack variant in mid-1987 with Lot 10, Block 23. The F/A-18D brought to the two-seat version the same modifications and improvements as the -C, along with a convertible aft cockpit to facilitate combat use of the -D for either pilot training or for a Weapons System Officer (WSO) in back instead of a pilot. The AFT Seat Kit allowed the aft cockpit to be configured with side controllers for combat missions and stick/throttle for pilot training. The first thirty-one builds of this new model were assigned to the Navy and Marine Corps training squadrons to replace the F/A-18B.

Night Attack Hornets Bring Forth New Capabilities

Beginning with Lot 12 in FY 1988, all production C/Ds were manufactured as fully night capable platforms and given the name Night Attack Hornets. Key to this upgrade was the GEC-Marconi AXS-9 (MXV-810) Cat Eyes night vision goggles (NVGs), two new Kaiser 5-inch by 5-inch color multi-functional displays (MFDs), and a Smiths Srs 2100 color digital moving map display. Raytheon's AAR-50 tactical navigation (NAVFLIR) provided all night attack models with night-time navigation imagery overlaid on the HUD. The AAR-50 pod, Thermal Imaging Navigation Set (TINS), was mounted on the right fuselage station and provided imagery that could be projected onto the HUD, but had no designation or tracking capability. The upgrade integrated the AAS-38A NITE Hawk FLIR (followed by the AAS-38B), which permitted self-designation of targets. A gold-tinted canopy was also added to help deflect radar and laser energy away from the cockpit.

The Night Attack F/A-18D models are used solely by the Marine Corps for all-weather attack aircraft, replacing the service's A-6E. Most modifications were to the aft cockpit, which formerly housed only a second set of flight controls. VMFA(AW)-121 received the first -D on May 11, 1990, and flew missions over Iraq

The F/A-18D is tactically a much-improved version of the F/A-18B developed for the United States Marine Corps. The two-seat D can be configured for flight training by installing a stick and throttle in the aft cockpit and is used in that manner by the Fleet Replacement Squadrons (FRS). The F/A-18D is used in operational squadrons only by the Marine Corps. *Jamie Hunter*

during Operation Desert Storm. The last F/A-18D was presented to VMFA(AW)-121 on August 25, 2000, marking the end of the Legacy Hornet production line.

Subsequent C/D Upgrades

The F404-GE-402 Enhanced Performance Engine (EPE), which produces 17,600 lb. thrust (78.48 kN) in afterburner, was designed for the Swiss, who sought more power for their Hornets, and later purchased by the Kuwaiti's. The Navy adopted the GE-402 engines for US models beginning with Lot 15 in FY 1992. Lot 13 Hornets and beyond also saw the incorporation of a GPS receiver in 1995 and Lot 16 saw the APG-73 radar upgrade. The APG-73 radar offered a better raid assessment mode, higher-resolution ground mapping modes, increased detection and tracking ranges, and a better ability to defeat enemy jamming. In 1997, another modification saw the standard APX-100 IFF (Identification Friend or Foe) replaced with an improved Hazeltine APX-113 Combined Interrogator Transponder (CIT). These are the row of five short blade antennas on the fighter's nose aft of the guns. The APX-113 features electronic beam steering that allows Hornet pilots to determine the range, bearing, and elevation of the interrogated aircraft. Kuwait was the first CIT customer, followed by US Hornets beginning with Lot 19 (165207 and up) in 1993.

The Phase I Radar Upgrade (RUG) APG-73 introduced in May 1994, brought with it significantly faster processing capabilities. The unit weighs the same as the APG-65, but offers a tenfold increase in processor speed, has greater memory, is easier to maintain, and is more reliable. Following its first flight on April 15, 1992, the APG-73 became standard on all production models (Lot 16, Block 43 and up) and the radars were retrofitted into older models. VFAs-146 and -147 were the first squadrons to receive the upgraded units. The APG-73 has the same operational modes as the APG-65, but the RUG Phase II (used only by Marine Corps F/A-18Ds) incorporated a high-resolution SAR for mapping during reconnaissance missions and autonomous targeting for the JSOW and JDAM weapons. It also allows tracking of up to twenty-four targets.

Hornets also received the on-board oxygen generating system (OBOGS) to replace the previous liquid oxygen (LOX) converter system, and replacement with Lot 13 in 1991 of the ASN-139 inertial navigation system (INS) with the ASN-39 laser-ring-gyro (LRG) system. ARC-210 radio provisions were added beginning in Lot 13 and 14, with the radios installed in Lot 17.

Reconnaissance Hornets

In 1982, McDonnell Douglas began work on a dedicated two-seat reconnaissance Hornet with a pod similar to the TARPS later developed for use by the F-14. Although quickly abandoned, what followed was a single-seat proposal, the F/A-18(R), which used a removable camera pallet installed in place of the M61A1 gun in the Hornet's nose. F/A-18A 160775 was modified to this configuration and first flew on August 15, 1984. While a viable option, the F/A-18(R) was never adopted. However, because the fate of the F/A-18 was still uncertain when the C/D models entered production, the nose sections were designed for easy eventual depot refit to the (R) configuration; these provisions were removed in "C" models beginning with Lot 12 in FY 1989.

The next reconnaissance version was the RF-18D for use by the Marines, which featured an all-weather Loral UPD-4 side-looking high-resolution synthetic aperture radar mounted on a centerline pod. Images would be viewable in the aft cockpit and data linked to ground stations in near real-time. This pod was successfully prototyped on an RF-4 in 1986, with deliveries planned beginning in 1990; however, the program was canceled as part of the defense drawdown at the end of the Cold War. The Marines then examined the Advanced Tactical Air Reconnaissance System (ATARS) developed by the Air Force for its F-16s, which utilized a pallet-mounted system similar to that used in the F/A-18(R). McDonnell Douglas began wiring its D variants to accommodate the pods beginning with Lot 14, Block 36, in anticipation of this capability. These fifty-two aircraft are designated as F/A-18D(RC).

ATARS uses the same cameras as the F/A-18(R), but adds a digital data-link pod for near-real-time transfer. ATARS is with the APG-73 RUG II upgrade to create reconnaissance strip maps and high resolution spot maps embedded with digital radar data. An initial contract was awarded on December 9, 1998. Although still in testing at the time, two ATARS-capable aircraft and three pallets were deployed by the Marine Corps during the Balkans conflict. ATARS was approved for full rate production in April 2000.

F/A-18A+ and A++

Some 200 F/A-18A/B aircraft were brought up to near F/A-18C standards. Known as F/A-18A+ and B+, changes were incorporated through ECP 560 (Navy) and ECP 583 (Marine Corps) beginning in the mid-1990s, and included improved processors and cockpit displays, APX-111 CIT, GPS navigation, SJU-17 NACES ejection seats, provisions for modern FLIRs, AIM-9X, and AIM-120. ECP 560 provided enhancements to the APG-65 radar, while ECP 583 upgraded to the APG-73. The Marine Corps undertook a second upgrade, adding ALE-47 chaff/flare dispensers, JHMCS, upgraded displays and digital maps, and MIDS/Link-16, and designated these as F/A-18A++.

An F/A-18C from VFA-82 *Marauders* makes an arrested landing aboard USS *Enterprise* (CVN-65) in June 2004, during Summer Pulse 2004, which involved the simultaneous deployment of seven aircraft carrier strike groups. *US Navy*

The Night Attack's gold tinted canopy was introduced in Lot 12 Hornets. An advanced bird strike windshield was also introduced beginning with Lot 18, Block 48, aircraft and up. *US Navy*

Introduced in production Lot 10, the F/A-18C Night Attack variant offered a significant improvement over the F/A-18A. This VFA-82 Hornet reveals some of the external differences introduced with the C model. These include the two small ECM antennas located just aft of the canopy, the slanted UHF/VHF blade antennae on the dorsal spine, an additional ALQ-67 RWR bulge just under the cockpit and ahead of the insignia marking, the upper RHAW antenna on the nose, and the gold tinted cockpit. The dome-shaped bulge behind the blade is the GPS antenna, introduced in Lot 17. An additional RWR antenna is present on the aft side of the vertical stabilizers. Most of the changes were internal. *US Navy*

The F404-GE-402 Enhanced Performance Engine (EPE) was ordered by the Swiss, put first delivered to the Kuwaitis in their F/A-18C/D purchase. The US Navy began installing wiring for the EPE in Lot 14, Block 36, and installation in Lot 15, Block 40 in roughly 1993. *Brad Elward*

A division of VFA-94 F/A-18C Hornets can be seen in formation over the Western Pacific in October 2003. The *Mighty Shrikes*, and her sister squadron VFA-97 *Warhawks*, were deployed with CVW-11 aboard USS *Nimitz* (CVN-68). VFA-94 and its sister squadron have been the only two Hornet squadrons to deploy overseas as part of the Marine Corps Unit Deployment Program (UDP), which assigns squadrons as expeditionary units (across the Pacific. *US Navy*

An F/A-18C from VFA-105 *Gunslingers* has its hook down as it prepares for entry into the landing pattern above the carrier USS *Harry S. Truman*. Transitioning from the LTV A-7 Corsair II, the *Gunslingers* received their F/A-18Cs in December 1990, and were assigned to the USS *John F. Kennedy* (CV-67), with whom they deployed in October 1992. VFA-105 deployed in support of Operations *Southern Watch* (1998, 2000), *Desert Fox* (1999), and *Iraqi Freedom* (2003). In July 2006, the squadron became the first East Coast Hornet squadron to transition to the F/A-18E Super Hornet (CVN-75). *US Navy*

All tactical F/A-18Ds are operated by the Marine Corps. A former A-6E Intruder squadron, VMFA(AW)-242 *Bats* transitioned to the F/A-18D beginning in December 1990. The squadron deployed to Al Asad AB, Iraq, in 2004–2005, where it provided air support for the 1st Marine Division during Operation *Phantom Fury* and also flew air cover during the Iraqi elections. This F/A-18D is armed with an AIM-120 ARMAAM on its outer wing station. *Ted Carlson*

The aft cockpit of the F/A-18D offers the Weapons System Officer (WSO) a similar presentation as seen by the pilot. Unlike the two-seat F/A-18F Super Hornet, the aft cockpit in the "D" model is not de-coupled, meaning that the pilot and WSO can use the radar independently. This center display shows a color moving map, while the left display mimics the pilots HUD and the right display shows the aircraft's weapons load. *Ted Carlson*

This daytime image shows the hand controllers of the F/A-18D aft cockpit, which allow the WSO to control weapons and sensor systems. F/A-18Ds often fly Forward Air Controller (Airborne) (FAC-A) missions, where they fly over the target area, designate targets, and call in close air support missions from other aircraft. *Ted Carlson*

The front cockpit of the two-seat F/A-18D looks exactly like the F/A-18C's cockpit. *Ted Carlson*

An excellent comparison photo of an F/A-18B (forefront) and F/A-18D (background) shows some of the physical differences between the aircraft. Notice the different antenna placement on the aircrafts' spine, tailfin, and forward fuselage. These Hornets belong to the Naval Strike and Air Warfare Center (NSAWC), now called the Naval Air Warfare Development Center (NAWDC). *Neil Pearson*

This forward fuselage image highlights the different antenna placement on an F/A-18C. The antenna near the "3" is not found on the F/A-18A; it is for the aircraft ALR-67 Radar Homing Warning Receiver (RWR) system. The rectangular blade antenna is for the UHF/IFF system, and the small cluster of antenna just forward of the blade is for the ALR-67. *Ted Carlson*

This F/A-18D from VMFA(AW)-225 carries three 330-gallon fuel tanks (stations 2, 5, 7), an AIM-9 Sidewinder (station 1), an ASQ-T50(V)2 Tactical Combat Training Systems (TCTS) pod (station 9), and two Mk.82 iron bombs (stations 2/8). The *Vikings* were reactivated in 1991 as an all-weather strike fighter squadron. *Jamie Hunter*

The F/A-18A-D Legacy Hornet uses the 330-gallon external fuel tank and can carry three—one each on the inner wing pylons and one on the centerline pylon. The Canadian Hornets also use the 480-gallon tank used by the F/A-18E/F Super Hornet. US Navy Hornets do not use these larger tanks because of the clearance required for carrier landings and because of the added stress and fatigue that would result from the larger tanks during carrier landings. Hornets usually fly combat missions with two tanks—mounted centerline station and station 7, or stations 3 and 7. Some also fly with a single centerline tank. *Ted Carlson*

The larger cockpit of the two-person F/A-18D requires a smaller Tank 1, reducing the aircraft's overall fuel by 316 gallons (2,150 lbs) of JP-5. *Jamie Hunter*

Three F/A-18D are shown here–VMFA(AW)-242 *Bats*; VMFA(AW)-225 *Vikings*, and VMFA(AW)-121 *Green Knights*. The *Green Knights* were the Marine Corps first F/A-18D squadron and flew during *Desert Storm*, posting 557 combat sorties and 1,655.5 combat flight hours. In 2012, the *Green Knights* began transition to the F-35B Lightening II. *US Navy*

A small number of F/A-18D were modified for the reconnaissance mission, receiving the Advanced Tactical Airborne Reconnaissance System (ATARS). Beginning with jet 164649, all "D" models were wired for the ATARS pallet. Today the Marine Corps operate about twelve such aircraft, three with each of the four (AW) squadrons. *US Navy*

The ATARS pallet replaces the gun in the aircraft's forward fuselage. It provides visual and infrared capability and features two digital tape recorders and a digital data link mounted in a centerline pod. The system works with the APG-73 Radar Upgrade (Phase II), which can record synthetic aperture radar (SAR) imagry. ATARS' first use occurred in 2000 when VMFA(AW)-332 *Moonlighters* deployed in support of Operation *Allied Force*. For some of these missions, *Moonlighter* ATARS Hornets would fly with two AIM-9 Sidewinders, two AIM-120 AMRAAM, two 330-gallon fuel tanks, an AGM-88 HARM, and an AAS-38 FLIR. *Ted Carlson*

"No Fly" Zones were enforced over northern and southern Iraq during the 1990s. This VFA-131 *Wildcat* F/A-18C is seen over Iraq in April 1996. It carries two AIM-120 AMRAAMs on its outer starboard wing station and an AIM-9 Sidewinder on each wingtip. At least two external tanks are also visible. *US Navy*

The laser-guided bomb became more and more important during the 1990s and 2000s, as the need to place munitions on an exact location became paramount. Here an F/A-18A from the Naval Air Warfare Center delivers a GBU-16 1,000-lb. Paveway II laser-guided bomb during a test to clear the weapon for fleet use. The GBU-16 is a Mk.83 iron bomb fitted with a laser-guidance unit and wings for guidance. *US Navy*

This view of an F/A-18C with VFA-147 *Argonauts* shows the gold tint canopy as well as several of the new antennas added to the Charlie model. *Brad Elward*

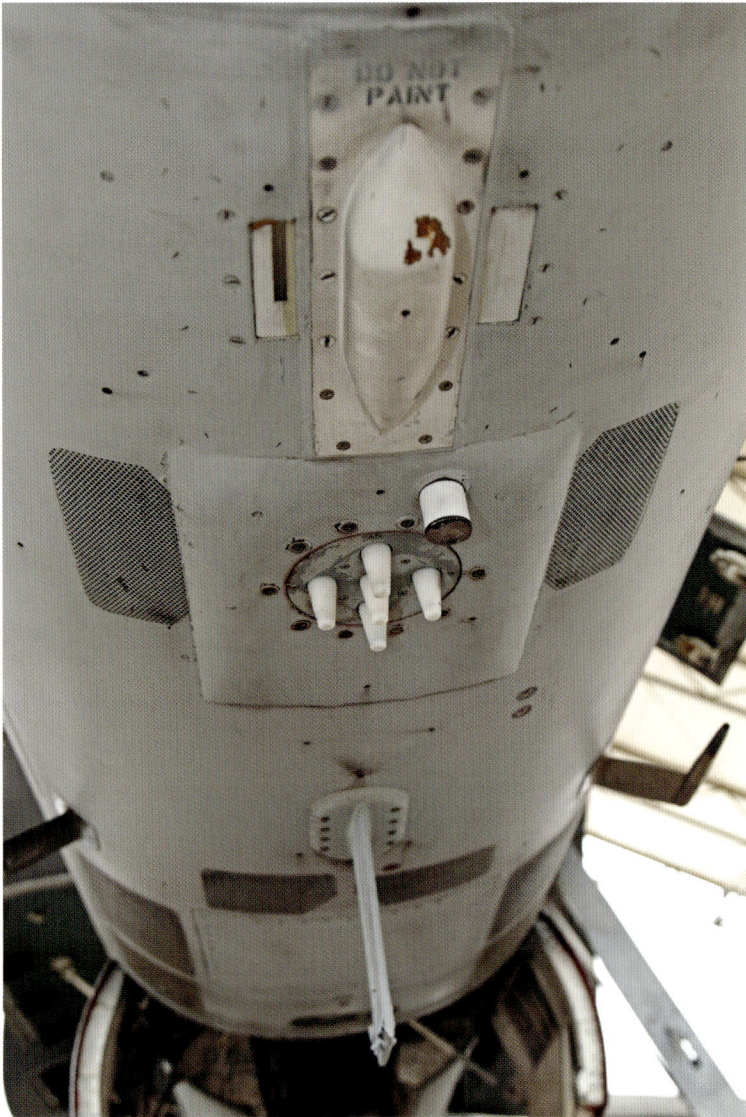

Just ahead of the UHF/IFF blade antenna is the five-antenna ALR-67 RWR. *Ted Carlson*

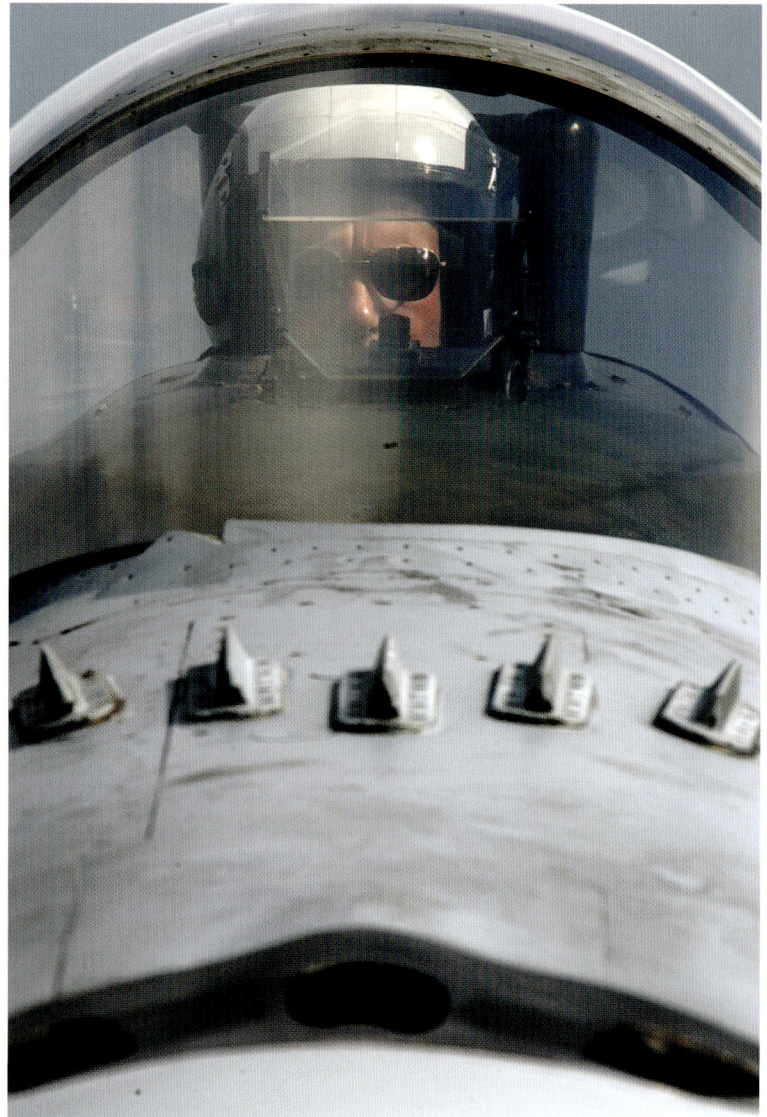

The five-blade APX-111X antennae was added to a number of F/A-18s as part of the Avionics Modernization Program. These are visible just ahead of the canopy but before the gun port. *US Navy*

The APG-73 radar replaced the APG-65 beginning in 1993 with Lot 16 as part of AFC-211.
Raytheon via Dennis Jenkins

F/A-18A-D production was divided into groups of aircraft referred to as Lots. Each Lot covered approximately one year of production, and the first deliveries of each new Lot commenced roughly the first of each October (federal Fiscal Year). Each Lot was further divided into groups known as production Blocks. Each Block was comprised of three Blocks of roughly equal size, with each Block translating to roughly four months of production. Major changes and new systems were implemented into the first Block of each Lot, and minor changes are implemented with the first aircraft of a Block that does not correspond with a new Lot. *Boeing*

VFA-15 *Valions* is based at NAS Oceana and currently operates the F/A-18C. The *Valions* transitioned to the Hornet in January 1987, and participated in Operation *Desert Storm* in 1991. The squadron's 2011 deployment aboard USS *George H.W. Bush* (CVN-77) saw it achieve a one hundred percent combat sortie completion rate while flying 430 missions in support of Operation Enduring Freedom and New Dawn. The *Valions* were disestablished in early 2017. *Dan Teker*

A VX-23 F/A-18C fires an AIM-9X Sidewinder in 1999. The *Salty Dogs* are based at NAS Patuxent River. The squadron performs research and testing on a variety of fixed-wing aircraft and performs weapons certification tests. The AIM-9X is a high-off bore site (HOBS) missile that, when used with the Joint Helmet Mounted Cueing System (JHMCS), can be aimed simply by the pilot looking at the target. The AIM-9X entered service in 2003. *Raytheon*

The F/A-18C/D tailfin looks slightly different than that of the F/A-18A/B; specifically, the antennas have been altered. These include, top to bottom, the ALQ-165 ECM high band, ALR-67 RWR, and ALQ-165 low band. The top position on the right stabilizer is a white navigation light. *Ted Carlson*

This F/A-18C from VFA-105 prepares to launch from the forward catapult of the USS *Harry S. Truman* (CVN-75) in November 2004. Notice the five-blade APX-111X antennas are not present. *US Navy*

The AGM-88 HARM is the Hornet's primary Suppression of Enemy Air Defense (SEAD) mission weapon. The HARM was developed as replacement to the AGM-45 Shrike and is a considerable upgrade. This VMFA-251 Hornet carries two HARM and two AIM-9 Sidewinder missiles, as well as a fuselage-mounted AIM-120 AMRAAM. Notice the off-set or asymmetrical external fuel tanks carried on stations 5 (centerline) and 7 (inner-wing). This configuration permits a clear field-of-view for the fuselage-mounted targeting pod carried on station 4. This Hornet is operating in the Arabian Gulf in 1998. *US Navy*

Only two aircraft in a Hornet squadron are authorized to wear high-visibility markings. One is the so-called "CAG Bird," Modex X00, which is the aircraft designated for the Commander of the Carrier Air Wing (CAG). The remaining squadron aircraft are painted two-tone gray. Shown here is Modex 400, the CAG aircraft of VFA-87 *Warhawks. Dan Teker*

This comparison (above and opposite) highlights the external differences between the forward fuselage and cockpit area of an F/A-18A (left) and F/A-18C (right). The "C" model has the additional ALR-67 antenna bubble on its nose by the Modex number and two ALQ-165 ECM antenna located just aft of the cockpit. Although only visible on the F/A-18C, the Charlie features a swept-angle UHF/VHF blade antenna. *Ted Carlson*

CHAPTER 5
Hornet Upgrades Beyond 2000

The F/A-18A+ represented an upgrade to the original A model, and included a substantial avionics and weapons system upgrade. VMFA-115 was the first Marine Corps squadron to receive the F/A-18A+. The *Silver Eagles* took their new aircraft on deployment in October 2002 aboard USS *Harry S. Truman* (CVN-75), and are shown here in 2005 in the Persian Gulf. VMFA-115 will transition to the F-35C in the early 2020s. *US Navy*

If the 1980s and 1990s marked the emergence and expansion of F/A-18A-D capabilities, the 2000s were the era of sustainment. Budget difficulties, heavy use in overseas operations, and delays associated with the Joint Strike Fighter (JSF) program stressed the strike fighter fleets and created a strike fighter shortfall of some 243 aircraft; recent estimates place this number at roughly sixty-five aircraft. As a result, the services sought to extend the Legacy Hornet service life beyond its original 6,000 flight hours, 2,000 arrested landings, and 8,300 total landings to a goal of 10,000 flight hours, with 17,000 landings and arrestments and 1,500 catapults.

The Navy began replacing fatigued arresting and catapult gear in late 2001. Within a few years, a formal Service Life Assessment Program (SLAP) began that evaluated fatigue-related issues and assessed the ability of the airframe to meet the stated life extension goals through a combination of inspections and airframe modifications. The program sought to determine whether the original demonstrated capability was able to meet the service lives given how the fleet actually operates. SLAP Phase 1 concentrated on structures primarily affected by arrestment, landing, and catapult loads; SLAP Phase 2 concentrated on the flight event driven structures. Planning began in the late 1990s; SLAP Phase 1 ran from late 2001 for approximately three years.

Legacy SLAP (2005–2008) was followed by a three-phased Service Life Extension Program (SLEP), which addressed the most critical airframe requirements. SLEP does not include capabilities upgrades; it only extends the airframe service life. SLEP was projected to be completed by 2012, but is now projected for completion in 2017. SLEP Phase A was a short-term program conducted in 2008 which reviewed the results of SLAP Phase 2 and developed notional repair concepts for locations not meeting the life extension goals.

SLEP Phase B was completed by late 2011, and updated the analysis tools to address some limitations identified in earlier analysis phases. SLEP Phase C is charged with completing life analysis for a variety of locations across the airframe and definition of retrofit concepts and associated ECPs which will allow continued operation to the end of the service life for those locations which have not met the SLEP life goals. SLEP Phase C will be completed in mid-2017.

The Navy also operates a High Flight Hour (HFH) inspection program to assess the material condition and airworthiness of F/A-18A-D to meet resourcing requirements as the aircraft reach 8,000 flight hours. The HFH program implemented a suite of inspections intended to assure structural integrity prior to implementing retrofits into the airframe. In addition, there were several stand-alone inspection bulletins on what were considered safety-of-flight structures. Since the SLEP effort had not yet begun, the inspection program was instituted to assure the safety of the airframe structure. The HFH Basic inspection bulletins were released in April 2009, however multiple verifications (2007–2008) were going on prior to release.

As of February 2016, 171 HFH inspections were successfully completed, with another 118 HFH inspections in-work. A Service Life Management Program (SLMP) monitors the overall health of the Legacy Hornet fleet through a complex analysis of inventories and management of aircraft usage rates at the squadron level. This program works in conjunction with the HFH inspections and the overall Legacy Hornet SLAP/SLEP programs. When SLEP kits are available, the HFH inspection will be eliminated.

In the early 2000s, the Navy began a Center Barrel Replacement Plus (CBR+) program to address fatigue issues and to replace the center fuselage section where the wings and main landing gear attach. The initial procedure was developed in 1991, and the program began in December 2000, well before SLAP and SLEP, to address concerns about the ability of the center fuselage structure to last as long as the inner wing structure. The one hundredth CBR+ aircraft, an F/A-18C for VMFA-323, was redelivered to the service in November 2011. By 2015, some 200 center barrel replacements had been completed.

The Legacy Hornet SLAP/SLEP and HFH has been successful, as of 2016, in achieving 8,000 flight hours for 171 aircraft and is well on the way to modifying an additional 150 Legacy Hornets to reach 10,000 hours. By early 2016, the Navy reported that ninety-one percent of the F/A-18A-D fleet had more than 6,000 flight hours, and nineteen percent (some 114 aircraft) had flown more than 8,000 flight hours. At the time, the highest flight hour airframe had more than 9,575 hours and was then forward-deployed.

The Navy and Marine Corps installed JHMCS, an AIM-9X missile capability, high order language mission computers, ALR-67v3 RWR, ALQ-214v5 Integrated Defensive Countermeasures (IDECM), night vision cueing and displays, radar enhancements, and MIDS-JTR on selected aircraft, as well as ATFLIR and Litening targeting pods. The Marine Corp further upgraded fifty-six Lot 7-9 F/A-18As, and thirty Lot 10/11 F/A-18Cs to a Lot 21 avionics standard with a tactical data link, digital communications, JHMCS, MIDS-JTR, and Litening pods.

In 2015, Boeing began upgrading some thirty F/A-18C Hornets previously consigned to desert storage (the "boneyard") for the Marine Corps. Part of the C+ Program, Boeing is modifying the avionics of these aircraft to a combat-ready condition at its facility in Cecil Field, Florida. The C+ Program is designed to upgrade a total of thirty C Model aircraft with AN/ALE-47 Countermeasures Dispensing System, Joint Helmet Mounted Cueing System (JHMCS), Multifunctional Information Distribution System (MIDS), Multi-purpose Display Group Upgrade (MDGU), including embedded Tactical Aircraft Moving Map Capability (TAMMAC), the Sixth Avionics Mux Bus, and APX-111 Combined Interrogator Transponder (CIT) for the USMC. Twenty-two of the thirty aircraft will be pulled from the "aircraft boneyard" in Arizona and will undergo a series of inspections and be reassembled for return-to-service. The remaining eight aircraft are existing fleet aircraft.

The process takes between nine and eighteen months per aircraft and should add roughly four years of service life (to a total of 8,000 hours) before the aircraft must undergo depot inspection. That translates to about 300 flight hours per year. The first C+ aircraft was inducted in 2014, and the last aircraft to be modified will be inducted in 2017. The program marked its first delivery in mid-2016, with 163755 delivered to VMFA-115.

When the 2000s began the Navy operated a combination of F/A-18A and -C aircraft in fleet squadrons, while the Marine Corps flew all types of Legacy Hornets. As the Super Hornet began entering Navy service in 2001, F/A-18As were replaced by Charlie models as squadrons transitioned to the F/A-18E, and many older A models were converted to F/A-18A+ standards. By the end of 2010, carrier air wings deployed with two Legacy Hornet squadrons, often one Navy and one Marine Corps. The existing Legacy Hornet inventory is approximately 609 aircraft in six Navy and eleven Marine Corps squadrons. In early 2016, it was projected that Legacy Hornets will continue in active squadrons until 2026, 2029 for Marine Corps active and reserve squadrons, and 2034 for Navy reserve squadrons.

A VMFA-115 F/A-18A+ catches a wire aboard USS *Harry S. Truman* (CVN-75) in 2004. The *Silver Eagles* were flying close-air support missions in support of Operation *Iraqi Freedom*. A few Navy squadrons, including VFA-97, also deployed with the F/A-18A+. *US Navy*

High Flight Hour (HFH) inspections are performed at several locations to assess the fatigue areas of Legacy Hornets as they approach and exceed 6,000 flight hours. The HFH inspections are intended to locate areas where repairs are needed to help extend the aircraft to 8,600 hours and as long as 10,000 hours. *Brad Elward*

VFA-113 *Stingers* CAG-bird sports a colorful "Bee" camouflage in early 2012 while deployed with CVW-17 aboard the USS *Carl Vinson* (CVN-70). *US Navy*

Introduced in 2003, the AIM-9X Sidewinder can be seen here being inspected pre-flight by the Hornet's pilot, who is wearing a flight helmet fitted with the Joint Helmet Mounted Cueing System (JHMCS). The F/A-18C was the lead Navy aircraft for the AIM-9X, which is also used on the F/A-18E/F. The JHMCS can also be used to designate ground targets. *Jamie Hunter*

Land-based Marine Corps Hornets began using the Northrop Grumman AAQ-28 Litening AT pod for navigation and multi-sensor targeting and surveillance. It is used by the Marine Corps F/A-18D squadrons, as well as the Australian, Finnish, and Spanish Hornets. Litening pods feature digital high-definition video, laser imaging, and forward-looking infrared detection. The pod is usually mounted on the aircraft's centerline station. *Jamie Hunter*

All US Navy Hornets and carrier-based Marine Corps Hornets now use the AAS-228 Advanced Targeting Forward-Looking Infrared (ATFLIR). The pod, mounted on the left fuselage station 4, integrates advanced EO and IR sensors with a powerful laser for designation. ATFLIR allows for sensor fusion and has automatic target recognition. ATFLIR can locate and designate targets day or night at ranges exceeding forty nautical miles and altitudes surpassing 50,000 feet. ATFLIR replaced the AAS-38A/B Nite Hawk, shown here as well. Canadian Hornets use the Lockheed Martin AAQ-33 Sniper targeting pod. *Ted Carlson*

Brad Elward

An F/A-18D from VMFA(AW)-225 *Vikings* starts into a left banking turn. The Hornet has an AIM-9X missile on the each wingtip and carries two 330-gallon external tanks on the inner pylons. An AAQ-28 Litening AT pod is mounted on the aircraft's centerline. *Jamie Hunter*

During the 2000s, the Joint Direct Attack Munition (JDAM) became the Hornets' weapon of choice. JDAM is a guidance kit that converts an unguided or "dumb" Mk.80 series bomb into an all-weather smart weapon. JDAM kits are given a GBU designation, which stands for Glide Bomb Unit, followed by a number. GBU-38/B are 500-lb. (225 kg) Mk.82; GBU-32(V)1/B are 1,000-lb. (450 kg) Mk.83; GBU-35(V)1/B are 1,000-lb. (450 kg) BLU-110; GBU-31(V)2/B are 2,000-lb. (900 kg) Mk.84; and GBU-31(V)4/B are 1,000-lb. (9800 kg) BLU-109 bombs. The GBU-54/B is a Mk.82 laser JDAM. The Marine Corps Hornet shown here has a JDAM on its starboard wing and two laser-guided Paveway II bombs on its port wing, giving the aircraft considerable flexibility in attacking targets. *US Navy*

The AGM-65 Maverick is an air-to-ground tactical missile used for close air support (CAS) against armor and other smaller-to-medium sized vehicles and structures. Mavericks can be optical, laser, or infrared-guided. This is an AGM-65E laser-guided Maverick and is seen on an F/A-18C from VFA-105. *US Navy*

A line of Hornets from VMFA-115 sit armed with AGM-65 Mavericks for upcoming missions during operations over Iraq in 2004. The last Hornet is from VFA-105. *US Navy*

The JHMCS can also be used to cue sensors to lock onto targets. Here a pilot wearing a JHMCS inspects a laser guided munition prior to his mission. *US Navy*

An F/A-18D from VMFA(AW)-225 drops four Mk.82 500-lb. (225 kg) high-drag "Snake-eye" bombs. The tailfins expand after jettison to permit low-altitude release and slow or "retard" the bomb so the deploying aircraft can safely exit the target area without sustaining damage from the explosions.
Ted Carlson

The *Checkerboards* of VMFA-312 currently fly the F/A-18C, shown here departing from USS *Harry S. Truman* (CVN-75) in 2014 is support of an Operation *Enduring Freedom* mission over Afghanistan. *US Navy*

VFA-125, the first Hornet FRS, closed its doors in October 2010, transitioning all remaining F/A-18 Legacy Hornet training to VFA-122, the F/A-18E/F Super Hornet FRS. The final Legacy Hornet departed NAS Lemoore in February 2016, and now all Navy Hornet training is conducted by VFA-106 at NAS Oceana. VFA-125 was recently stood up as the West Coast F-35C FRS. *US Navy*

The Hornet wasted no time getting into action. Hornet squadrons often escorted Soviet bombers such as this F/A-18A from VFMA-323 *Death Rattlers* flying next to a Tu-16 "Badger" bomber in early 1986. The squadron was deployed aboard USS *Coral Sea* (CV-43). *US Navy*

The F/A-18's combat debut occurred in 1986, when four Hornet squadrons from the aircraft carrier USS *Coral Sea* (CV-43) provided support for the US air strikes against Libya. Operation *Prairie Fire* ran from March 24, to April 14, 1986, and was directed against Libyan surface-to-air and radar sites. The *El Dorado Canyon* raid occurred on the night of April 14-15, and involved Hornets from VFAs-131 and -132, and VMFAs-314 and -323. Twenty F/A-18As participated in the raids against Libya, all launched from the *Coral Sea*. Some were armed with AGM-88 HARM, which were launched against air-defense radars, while another group was aloft carrying air-to-air and anti-shipping harpoon missiles, protecting the task force from missile-firing surface ships. Another contingency of Hornets was held in reserve for additional air-to-air protection.

During the forty-two-day air campaign of Operation *Desert Storm* that began on January 17, 1991, Hornets from nine Navy and seven Marine Corps F/A-18 squadrons flew a variety of missions, with most Navy missions divided roughly equally between strike, general support, and fleet defense. Approximately thirty Canadian CF-18 Hornets also flew in support of *Desert Storm*, logging a total of 5,730 flight hours, including 2,700 combat air patrol sorties, with no losses. Canadian Hornets flew a variety of combat air patrols, escort, and strike missions, and even delivered a small number of laser-guided munitions with the help of US Navy A-6E Intruders. The CF-18s flew fifty-six bombing sorties during the one hundred-day ground war.

Hornet missions early in the war consisted of strike escort and fleet defense, but these soon switched to strike missions as air superiority was obtained. Marine Corps missions focused almost exclusively on close air support (eighty-four percent). VMFA(AW)-121's F/A-18Ds were heavily tasked in the FAC role. While Hornets used a variety of ordnance, most of the munitions delivered, some 11,179, were unguided weapons; only 368 guided munitions were delivered by Hornets. Weapons included Mk.80 series iron bombs, AGM-62 Walleye, AGM-84E SLAM, AGM-65 Maverick, AGM-88 HARM, and Zuni rockets.

By the war's end, Hornets had accumulated 11,000 sorties and more than 30,000 flight hours. Total tonnage delivered amounted to 5,513 tons, although this averaged only 0.74 tons per day per plane. One of the biggest drawbacks was the airframes lack of an organic laser designator, forcing most Hornets to either drop unguided bombs or to pair with a laser-equipped A-6E or A-7E. Despite the high number of missions, only two Hornets were lost and eight damaged, one was so severely damaged that it flew thirty-five minutes without oil pressure.

Perhaps the Hornet's defining moment of the war occurred on January 17, when two F/A-18s from USS *Saratoga* (CV-60) shot down two Iraqi MiG-21 fighters while the Hornets were en route to attack airfield H3 in western Iraq. Each Hornet was armed with two AIM-7 Sparrows, two AIM-9 Sidewinders, a 330 gallon (1,249.2 liter) centerline tank, and four 2,000 lb. (907.2 kg) Mk.84

bombs. Without jettisoning their bomb load, then-LCdr. Mark Fox, who later became a vice admiral, shot down one Iraqi MiG with an AIM-9, while Lt. Nick Mongillo achieved his kill with an AIM-7, although he fired one Sparrow that failed to track. Fox piloted F/A-18C 163508/AA-401 and Mongillo flew in F/A-18C 163502/AA-410. The engagement, from first warning to kill, took less than one minute. Both men then went on to complete their mission and successfully bombed their respective targets.

Hornets continued to play an important role in post-Gulf War conflicts, including Bosnia in 1995, Kosovo in 1999, various *Northern* (1991) and *Southern Watch* (1992) *No-Fly Zone* operations, and the *Enduring Freedom* and *Iraqi Freedom* campaigns in the early 2000s. In Bosnia, VMFA(AW)-533 flew SEAD and Close Air Support (CAS) missions joined by Hornets aboard USS *Theodore Roosevelt* (CVN-71) and *America* (CV-66). During the Bosnian conflict, VMFA(AW)-533 flew more than one hundred strike sorties. Hornets from Spain and Canada were also committed. Spain's fleet of EF-18s flew more than 14,000 flight hours during their five-year deployment in support of Allied air operations in and around Bosnia and Kosovo.

Marine Corps F/A-18D squadrons VMFA(AW)-332 and -533 saw action during Kosovo operations, along with F/A-18Cs from VFAs-15 and -87 aboard *Roosevelt*. Again, Hornets flew a large number of SEAD missions. Throughout both conflicts, most missions saw Hornets carry two AIM-9 Sidewinders and an AIM-120 AMRAAM for air threats, and a GBU-16 1,000-lb. bomb and HARM for use against ground targets. The two-seat F/A-18Ds were also proficient at CAS and Forward Air Control (FAC) and were, for a time during the conflict, the only Hornets allowed to make strike missions because of the perception that with two crewmembers, they were less likely to release a weapon on friendly (blue) forces.

In the 1991 Gulf War, Marine Corps F/A-18Ds flew both attack and FAC-Airborne missions over geographic grid "kill" boxes. The aircraft were also active in support of United Nations operations over Bosnia and Kosovo. During the spring 1999 *Allied Force* air campaign against Yugoslavia, two Marine F/A-18D(RC)s from VFMA(AW)-332 deployed to Tazar, Hungary, with their new ATARS reconnaissance system and flew combined reconnaissance/strike missions against Yugoslavian forces.

Even with these successes, the Hornet's most important contributions were yet to come. Following the terrorist attacks of September 11, 2001, US Navy F/A-18 Hornets flew CAS missions in support of Operation *Enduring Freedom* in Afghanistan. Air operations began on October 7, 2001, and by the end of the first three months of the war, carrier-based Navy and Marine Corps F/A-18 Hornets had flown more than 3,700 strike sorties. Indeed, Hornets bore the brunt of the air missions, flying more than one-half of all combat strike sorties and 2,500 more than the next most utilized aircraft, the F-14.

Operation *Iraqi Freedom*, which began on March 21, 2003, saw some 250 Hornets, including eighty-four USMC Hornets and fourteen RAAF Hornets fly a variety of strikes in what became known as the "Hornet War." Four carriers, with ten Hornet squadrons embarked, were stationed in the Northern Arabian Sea, while two carriers with six Hornet squadrons were stationed in the eastern Mediterranean Sea. An entire Marine Air Wing, MAG-11, with seven Hornet squadrons was based at Al Jaber, Kuwait; some F/A-18D were ATARS-capable.

USS *Coral Sea* (CV-43) deployed with four F/A-18 squadrons in 1985–86. Here, VMFA-314 warns off a Libyan MiG-23 "Flogger" somewhere over the Mediterranean Sea. *US Navy*

An AIM-7 Sparrow air-to-air missile is being loaded onto a VFA-132 F/A-18A Hornet in 1989. The Sparrow was the Hornet's medium-range missile until replaced by the AIM-120 AMRAAM in the mid-1990s. This image gives a good look at the splitter plate between the engine intakes and the Hornet's fuselage. *US Navy*

The carrier *Coral Sea* took the Hornet into its first combat during Operation *El Dorado Canyon* in 1986. Hornets flew Suppression of Enemy Air Defense (SEAD) missions armed with AGM-88 HARMS, Combat Air Patrol (CAP) missions, and anti-surface patrols while air wing intruders struck targets in Libya. The Hornets' performance was deemed exceptional. *US Navy*

By the 2000s, the AIM-120 AMRAAM had completely replaced the AIM-7 Sparrow as the Navy's medium-range air-to-air missile. Here two AIM-120s are mounted on an LAU-127/A launch rail. *US Navy*

The AIM-9 Sidewinder serves as the Hornet's close-range air-to-air missile. An AIM-9M is shown here mounted on an LAU-7 launch rail on the aircraft's wingtip station, while a GBU-12 500-lb. (225 kg) laser-guided bomb can be seen in the background. *US Navy*

Hornets carried the AIM-7 until 1992. This Hornet from VFA-136 *Knighthawks* launches a Sparrow at a drone in the Northern Arabian Gulf just weeks before the onset of Operation *Desert Storm. US Navy*

Two Hornets from VMFA-323 armed with Paveway II laser-guided bombs fly over the Gulf of Sidra in early 1986, just months before the *El Dorado Canyon* operation. *US Navy*

Hornets flew close air support and SEAD missions during *Desert Storm*. Here, an F/A-18A from VMFA-235 is armed with two AGM-88 HARMs, two AIM-7 Sparrow, and two AIM-9 Sidewinders, and three external 330-gallon fuel tanks. The squadron deployed to Shaikh Isa Air Base, Bahrain, on August 22, 1990, and was the first fighter squadron in theater during Operation *Desert Shield*. The *Death Angels* flew over 2,800 sorties during Operation *Desert Storm*. US Navy

Then-LCdr, Mark Fox of VFA-81 *Sunliners* stands on his aircraft's ladder following his shoot-down of a MiG-21 on January 17, 1991. Lt. Nick Mongillo of the same squadron also downed a MiG-21 that same day. Fox and Mongillo were en route to a target near airfield H3 armed with four Mk.83 bombs and an air-to-air missile complement. One F/A-18 was lost that evening, thought to be the victim of a MiG-25PD. *US Navy*

An F/A-18C Hornet from VFA-147 *Argonauts* flies over burning oil fields near Kuwait City during a *Southern Watch* mission in 1993. The *Argonauts* transitioned from the A-7 Corsair II. *US Navy*

This VMFA-235 F/A-18C flies over Iraq in March 1991, carrying a weapons load similar to that carried by Fox and Mongillo on their January 17, MiG kill mission. *US Navy*

The *Bengals* of VMFA(AW)-224 deployed to Aviano, Italy, in mid-1994 as part of the Operation *Deny Flight* operations over Bosnia–Herzegovina. The *Bengals* flew 1,150 sorties for 3,485 flight hours, 1,150 of which were at night. The squadron returned to Aviano in September 1995, to support NATO Operation *Deliberate Force*. This F/A-18D carries a flexible swing load consisting of an AGM-65 Maverick and laser-guided bomb on its wings, and a Mk.82 500-lb. (225 kg) iron bomb on its centerline pylon. *Boeing*

A Hornet from the *Wildcats* of VFA-131 patrols over the Arabian Gulf in 1996 during Operation *Southern Watch*, enforcing the "No Fly" Zone over southern Iraq. *US Navy*

NAS Fallon is the home of the Navy's Fighter Weapons School (TOPGUN) and Strike. Both have a small cadre of F/A-18As that fly against students and visiting air wings. *Ted Carlson*

Two GBU-12 500-lb. (225 kg) laser-guided bombs are on the wing on this VFA-94 *Mighty Shrikes* Hornet during a mission over Afghanistan during Operation *Enduring Freedom* (OEF) in October 2001. The squadron was with CVW-11 aboard USS *Carl Vinson* (CVN-70). *US Navy*

Aerial refueling was crucial to long-distance missions over Afghanistan. Hornets would depart carriers located in the Indian Ocean for missions lasting as long as seven to nine hours. This Hornet carries three LGMs, an AAS-38 Nite Hawk pod on fuselage station 4, an ASQ-173 TLFIR on fuselage station 6, and two wingtip Sidewinders, plus a right wing and centerline external fuel tank. *US Navy*

A Lot 12 F/A-18C from VFA-94 carries a JDAM GPS-guided bomb on an OEF mission in early November 2001. *US Navy*

This VFA-137 *Kestrels* Charlie model taxis on the carrier deck with an AGM-65 Maverick on the outboard wing station and an AIM-9M Sidewinder on the outer launch rail during *Iraqi Freedom* operations in March 2003. *US Navy*

A VFA-15 *Valions* F/A-18C is seen launching from USS *Theodore Roosevelt* (CVN-71). This Hornet is armed with an AIM-120 AMRAAM and carries at least two external fuel tanks. *US Navy*

Two F/A-18C Hornets, one from Marine Corps squadron VMFA-323, and one from Navy squadron VFA-137, prepare to launch off the waste catapult aboard USS *Constellation* (CV-64) in March 2003. Both aircraft are carrying BDU-5 bombs designed to explode and disburse informational leaflets to the Iraqi people and military forces. Hornets dropped leaflets on twenty-four separate missions beginning March 9. *US Navy*

Most Hornets did not carry much of an air-to-air weapons load, given the lack of any significant air threat over Iraq or Afghanistan. This VFA-195 *Dambusters* F/A-18C carries at least three AIM-120 air-to-air missiles and two external tanks. *US Navy*

A Hornet armed with a flex load carries, from top to bottom, an AGM-65 Maverick, two external fuel tanks, a Nite Hawk FLIR, a GBU-32 1,000-lb. (450 kg) JDAM, and a 1,000-lb. (450 kg) GBU-16. *US Navy*

An F/A-18D assigned to the *Knighthawks* of Marine Fighter Attack Squadron Five Three Three (VMFA-533) taxis on the flight line in Al Assad AB, Iraq. VMFA-533 was deployed with 1st Marine Expeditionary Force (IMEF) in support of global war on terrorism. *US Marine Corps*

Hornets fired a number of AGM-88 HARM against Iraqi air defense sites during *Desert Storm*, as well as other operations in Iraq between 1991 and 2005. Four hundred eight were launched by US air forces during *Iraqi Freedom*. *US Navy*

A Hornet pilot from VFA-113 *Stingers* makes his way to the target on the opening night of Operation *Iraqi Freedom* in 2003. F/A-18A Hornets managed a 79.6 percent Mission Capable (MC) rate while F/A-18Cs posted an 87.3 percent MC rate. *US Navy*

The *Green Knights* of VMFA(AW)-121 were the first F/A-18D squadron to deploy and the first to enter combat. The squadron made its debut in Operation *Desert Storm. Boeing*

Canadian CF-18As made significant contributions to the air offensive over Libya during the 2011 NATO-led Operation *United Protector* (OUP). Six CF-18s deployed out of Trapani Air Base, Italy, and flew 946 sorties (ten percent of NATO strikes), dropping 696 bombs, many of which were laser-guided Paveway II munitions as shown here. *Gert Kromhout*

A CF-18A takes on fuel from a tanker during Operation *United Protector*. An AGM-88 HARM and GBU-12 500-lb. (225 kg) can be seen on this aircraft as well as an external fuel tank on the right inner wing station. *Gert Kromhout*

APPENDIX
US Navy and Marine Corps Hornet Operators

United States Navy

US Navy Hornet operational squadrons are split between the East and West Coast. East Coast squadrons were based at NAS Cecil Field, Florida, from 1984 through 1999, when the strike fighter community was relocated to NAS Oceana, Virginia. The West Coast squadrons are based at NAS Lemoore, California, with forward deployed squadrons based at NAF Atsugi, Japan. The chart below lists the squadron's primary location during their operational use of the F/A-18 Classic Hornet.

VFA-106 *Gladiators* and -125 *Rough Raiders* are the type Fleet Replenishment Squadrons (FRS). Several of the initial East Coast squadrons were established or transitioned at NAS Lemoore before being relocated to Cecil Field in 1985. Forward-deployed strike fighter squadrons are based at NAF Atsugi, Japan, and are part of CVW-5. VFA-125 was the first Navy squadron to receive the Hornet and VFA-113 *Stingers* and VFA-25 *Fists of the Fleet* were the first fleet squadrons to transition.

Squadron	Name	Based At	Operational Dates	Aircraft
VFA-15	*Valions*	Cecil Field/Oceana	1986–2017	F/A-18A/C
VFA-22	*Fighting Redcocks*	Lemoore	1990–2004 (E)	F/A-18C
VFA-25	*Fists of the Fleet*	Lemoore	1983–2012 (E)	F/A-18A/C
VFA-27	*Chargers/Royal Maces*	Lemoore/Atsugi	1991–2004 (E)	F/A-18C
VFA-34	*Blue Blasters*	Cecil Field/Oceana	1996–Present	F/A-18A/C
VFA-37	*Bulls*	Cecil Field/Oceana	1990–Present	F/A-18A/C
VFA-81	*Sunliners*	Cecil Field/Oceana	1988–2008 (E)	F/A-18C
VFA-82	*Marauders*	Cecil Field/Oceana/MCAS Beaufort	1987–2005	F/A-18C
VFA-83	*Rampagers*	Cecil Field/Oceana	1988–Present	F/A-18C
VFA-86	*Sidewinders*	Cecil Field/Oceana	1987–2011 (E)	F/A-18C
VFA-87	*Golden Warriors*	Cecil Field/Oceana	1986–2016 (E)	F/A-18A/C/A+
VFA-94	*Mighty Shrikes*	Lemoore	1990–2015 (F)	F/A-18C
VFA-97	*Warhawks*	Lemoore	1991–2013 (E)	F/A-18A/C/A+
VFA-105	*Gunslingers*	Cecil Field/Oceana	1990–2006 (E)	F/A-18C
VFA-106	*Gladiators*	Cecil Field/Oceana	1984–Present	F/A-18A-D
VFA-113	*Stingers*	Lemoore	1984–2016 (E)	F/A-18A/C

Squadron	Name	Based At	Operational Dates	Aircraft
VFA-125	Rough Raiders	Lemoore	1980–2010	F/A-18A-D
VFA-127	Desert Bogies/Cyclons	Lemoore	1992–1996	F/A-18A
VFA-131	Wildcats	Cecil Field/Oceana	1983–Present	F/A-18A/C
VFA-132	Privateers	Cecil Field	1984–1992	F/A-18A
VFA-136	Knight Hawks	Cecil Field/Oceana	1985–2010 (E)	F/A-18A/C
VFA-137	Kestrels	Lemoore	1985–2003 (E)	F/A-18A/C
VFA-146	Blue Diamonds	Lemoore	1989–2015 (E)	F/A-18A/C
VFA-147	Argonauts	Lemoore	1989–2007 (E)	F/A-18A/C
VFA-151	Vigilantes	Atsugi	1986–2013 (E)	F/A-18C
VFA-161	Chargers	Cecil Field	1986 - 1987	F/A-18A
VFA-192	World Famous Golden Dragons	Atsugi	1986–2014 (E)	F/A-18A/C
VFA-195	Dam Busters	Atsugi	1985–2010 (E)	F/A-18A/
VFA-201*	Hunters	Ft. Worth, TX	1999–2007	F/A-18A
VFA-203*	Blue Dolphins	Jacksonville, FL/Atlanta, GA	1989–2004	F/A-18A
VFA-204*	River Rattlers	New Orleans, LA	1991–Present	F/A-18A
VFA-303*	Golden Hawks	Lemoore	1984–1994	F/A-18A
VFA-305*	Lobos	Point Mugu, CA	1987–1994	F/A-18A
VFC-12**	Fighting Omars	Oceana	1994–Present	F/A-18A/B/A+/C
VFC-13**	Saints	Fallon	1992–1996	F/A-18A
VX-4	Evaluators	Point Mugu, CA	1981–1994	F/A-18A-D
VX-5	Vampires	China Lake	1982–1994	F/A-18A/B
VX-9	Vampires	China Lake	1994–Present	F/A-18A-D
VX-23	Dust Devils	Patuxent River, MD	1991–Present	F/A-18C/D
VF-45	Blackbirds			F/A-18A
VAQ-34	Electric Horsemen	Lemoore	1991–1993	F/A-18B
NAWC		Fallon		F/A-18A
NFWS		Miramar/Fallon		F/A-18A
NASA		Edwards AFB		F/A-18A
Naval Weapons Center		China Lake, CA		F/A-18A
Pacific Missile Test Center		Point Mugu, CA		F/A-18A
USN Flight Demonstration Team	Blue Angels	Pensacola, FL	1986	F/A-18A/B

* = Reserve squadron.

** = Adversary/composite

(E) = Transitioned to F/A-18E

(F) = Transitioned to F/A-18F

NAWC = Naval Air Warfare Center (now Naval Air Training and Development Center)

United States Marine Corps

The initial cadre of Marine Corps Hornet squadrons transitioned with the Navy's VFA-125 at NAS Lemoore. Soon, however, VMFAT-101 Sharpshooters became the Marines' Fleet Replenishment Squadron (FRS) and set up shop at MCAS El Toro. For the majority of the Hornet's long career, Marine Corps F/A-18s were based stateside at MCAS Cherry Point, North Carolina; MCAS Beaufort, South Carolina; and MCAS El Toro, California; and overseas at MCAS Kaneohe Bay Hawaii, and MCAS Iwakuni, Japan.

Squadron	Name	Based At	Operational Dates	Aircraft
VMFAT-101	Sharpshooters	El Toro/Miramar	1987–Present	F/A-18A-D
VMFA-112*	Cowboys	Ft. Worth, TX	1992–Present*	F/A-18A/A+
VMFA-115	Silver Eagles	Beaufort	1985–2020[1]	F/A-18A/A+
VMFA-122	Werewolves	Beaufort	1986–Present[2]	F/A-18A/C
VMFA-134*	Hawks	Miramar	1983–2007	F/A-18A
VMFA-142	Flying Gators	Ft. Worth	1990–2008	F/A-18A
VMFA-212	Lancers	MCB Hawaii	1988–2008[3]	F/A-18C
VMFA-232	Red Devils	MCB Hawaii/Miramar	1988–Present	F/A-18C/D
VMFA-235	Death Angels	MCB Hawaii/El Toro/Miramar	1989–1996	F/A-18C
VMFA-251	Thunderbolts	Beaufort	1986–Present	F/A-18A/C
VMFA-312	Checkerboards	Beaufort	1987–Present	F/A-18A
VMFA-314	Black Knights	Miramar	1982–Present	F/A-18A/C
VMFA-321*	Hell's Angels	Cherry Point	1991–2011	F/A-18C
VMFA-323	Death Rattlers	Miramar	1982–Present	F/A-18A/C
VMFA-333	Shamrocks	Beaufort	1987–1992	F/A-18A
VMFA-451	Warlords	Beaufort	1987–1997[4]	F/A-18A
VMFA-531	Grey Ghosts	Cherry Point	1984–1992	F/A-18A
VMFA(AW)-121	Green Knights	Cherry Point/Miramar	1989–2012 (J)	F/A-18D
VMFA(AW)-224	Bengals	Beaufort	1993–Present	F/A-18D
VMFA(AW)-225	Vikings	Miramar	1991–Present	F/A-18D
VMFA(AW)-242	Batmen	Iwakuni	1990–Present	F/A-18D
VMFA(AW)-332	Moonlighters	Beaufort	1993–2007	F/A-18D
VMFA(AW)-533	Hawks	Beaufort	1992–Present	F/A-18D

* = Reserve squadron.

(J) = Transitioned to F-35B

[1] = Set to transition to F-35C in 2020

[2] = In cadre status and set to transition to F-35B in 2018

[3] = Set to transition to MV-22B squadron in 2019

[4] = Became VMFAT-501 to become USMC F-35B FRS